101

questions your
cat would ask

?

101
questions

What's bothering your cat and how

?

to solve its problems

your cat would ask

Honor Head

Consulting veterinarian:
Helen Dennis VetMB MRCVS

METRO BOOKS
NEW YORK

Metro Books
122 Fifth Avenue
New York, NY10011

ISBN: 978-0-7607-7283-6

Printed in Singapore

5 7 9 10 8 6 4

Contents

1 Training your Cat 8

2 Feeding your Cat 30

Introduction   6

Introduction

As any cat owner will tell you, cats can be affectionate, funny, demanding, and capricious. As any cat will tell you, cat owners can be affectionate, funny, demanding, and capricious, and sometimes learning to live together is not so easy. The **101 questions** in this book are asked from the cat's point of view, and were carefully selected to provide information and guidance to owners on the main areas that affect a cat's well-being — training, feeding, and caring for the cat, and understanding its behavior.

Sharing your home with a cat or two is a joyous experience, but learning to understand your cat's basic needs and behavior patterns will result in a closer and more rewarding relationship. With a little patience, thoughtfulness, and foresight any owner can provide a happier and healthier environment for his or her cat. In return, the cat will give its affection and companionship. So, read on to discover **101 questions** your cat might ask to help you understand and appreciate why cats are among the most fascinating, infuriating, and lovable of creatures.

? ? ? ? ? ? ? ? ? ?

Why is it so important to handle me correctly

How should I be carried on a car journey

How are you going to train me to use a litterbox

Why have I started to soil in the house

Why do some cats urinate in the bathtub instead of in their litterbox

How do I know which part of the yard to use as a bathroom

SPECIAL FEATURE: Training a kitten

Why can't I scratch the furniture

Why can't I scrounge a few tidbits from your dinner guests

Do I have to wear a collar

Training your Cat

A well-trained, easy-to-handle cat is a pleasure to live with. Knowing how to introduce a kitten or cat into your home, how to housetrain it quickly and effectively, and how to handle the cat with care and respect, will help you and your pet to live together in peace and harmony.

It is almost impossible to resist picking a cat up, and doing this properly, with care and respect, will result in a relaxed and secure relationship between owner and pet. There are times when it is particularly important that a cat feels confident being handled by its owner, such as when it is sick or injured, or receiving medicine.

? *When* *I was a kitten, I was picked up by the scruff. Is this still OK now that I'm older?*

The straight answer to this is no! Not only would an adult cat find this way of being picked up very uncomfortable, but it could put undue strain on the cat's neck muscles. Mother cats carry their kittens by the scruff when they are tiny and weigh very little. But after the first few weeks, this way of carrying a cat could be dangerous – to both cat and owner! However, most cats love to be picked up and cuddled, and humans love to do it. If it is done in the right way, both will enjoy the experience.

why is it so important

? *So what is the best way to pick me up?*

The most comfortable way is to put one hand around the cat's body under its front legs, and to scoop up the back legs with the other hand. The cat should be held securely without squeezing, and its hindquarters always supported. Never leave its back legs dangling, because this could strain the spine and is uncomfortable for the cat. Never grab at a cat and force it to be picked up, or squeeze it too tightly around its middle. Always supervise children when they pick up cats.

to handle me correctly ?

Sitting Comfortably

Once the cat is held securely and feels relaxed, it will find its own way to sit comfortably.

Cats like to be held, and from this vantage point, many like to peer over your shoulder to see what is happening behind your back. Always make sure its bottom and back legs are well supported, and hold it firmly without squeezing.

Not all cats like to be cradled like a baby. If you find one that does, make sure it is held securely and is well supported. If a cat doesn't like to be held like this, don't force it.

When the cat is ready to get down, don't force it to stay. Still supporting its body, place it gently on the floor. Don't let it roll out of your arms – for a cat this is a bit like falling out of bed!

A

Without doubt, in a crate! Even if a cat is happy to travel sitting on the car seat or in the back window, this should be avoided. A cat loose in a car is a potential danger to the human travelers, and could also suffer serious injury itself. A sudden swerve or braking could cause bad bruising if the cat hits the floor or the sides of the car. A sudden unavoidable movement might cause the cat to panic. It might get under the driver's feet so that the pedals cannot be operated, or it might leap into the driver's lap. Even if the journey is completed safely, the cat may dash out through an open car door or window when it has reached its destination, and if the area is unfamiliar or dangerous, the cat may be lost forever.

Q. How should I be carried on a car journey

? *So how are you going to get me into the crate?*

It's one of those inexplicable cat facts of life that while most cats cannot resist jumping into a box half their size and refusing to get out, they would rather be stuck up a tree in the middle of a pack of baying hounds than be in the same room as a cat crate! To help get the cat accustomed to the crate, leave it standing open for a couple of days before the trip. Let the cat investigate the crate at its leisure. Put a favorite blanket or toy in the crate, so that the cat feels it is part of its normal living space. If, on the day, the cat puts up a huge struggle, wrap it in a towel or other soft cloth to provide protection from scratching, and place it gently but firmly in the crate. Try not to squeeze or push, since this might cause an injury, and talk to the cat soothingly.

? *Will I get car sick?*

Cats don't usually suffer from motion sickness, but may experience symptoms such as excessive salivation and panting. To help avoid this, don't give the cat any food for six to eight hours before the journey, and no liquid for one to two hours beforehand. Sedatives and motion sickness pills can be prescribed by a veterinarian. Never give the cat human medication.

Best Baskets

If you plan frequent trips with your cat, it is worth investing in a strong, reliable carrying container.

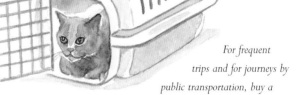

For frequent trips and for journeys by public transportation, buy a solid and secure fiberglass or polyethylene carrier. These are easy to clean, allow the cat to see and be seen, and are strong and escape-proof.

For a kitten, or an elderly or sedate cat, a cardboard cat box may be suitable for a short trip. However, most healthy adult cats will soon tear and chew their way through this type of container.

Old-fashioned wicker cat carriers may be suitable for short car journeys, but they are drafty, difficult to clean, and the doors and fastenings sometimes become loose, making them less secure than their modern counterparts.

Q. How are you going to

A Cats are by nature clean and fastidious, so training a kitten to use a litterbox should not be difficult. Kittens should be taught to use the box when they are about three to four weeks of age. The litterbox should be placed in a quiet, secluded corner where the kitten won't be disturbed. Make sure that there is enough litter in the box for the kitten to scratch a hole and cover it over again. Place the kitten gently in the box, and let it get used to the smell and feel of the litter.

At first, the kitten may not know how to use the box, and it may soil elsewhere in the house. Don't shout at the kitten, and never rub its nose in the mess – the smell will only encourage it to use this spot again. Simply say "No!" in a firm but quiet voice, and place the kitten in the box. Establish a routine of putting the kitten in the box after it has eaten, because eating prompts the kitten to move its bowels almost immediately. Never place the box near a cat's food. If the kitten continually refuses to use the box, move it to another spot and try using a different litter.

train me to use a litterbox?

? *What about an adult cat?*

A fully grown adult cat may take a little longer to train to use a litterbox than a kitten, but training is not impossible. The method of training a grown cat is the same as for a kitten – show the cat where the box is, and keep placing the cat gently in the box when it looks ready to use it.

Litterbox Etiquette

Once you have trained your kitten or cat to use a litterbox, always keep it clean and the litter fresh.

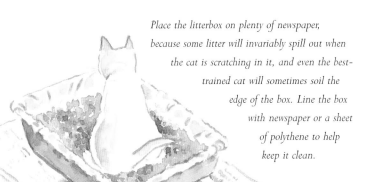

Place the litterbox on plenty of newspaper, because some litter will invariably spill out when the cat is scratching in it, and even the best-trained cat will sometimes soil the edge of the box. Line the box with newspaper or a sheet of polythene to help keep it clean.

Timid cats who feel especially vulnerable might like to use a covered litterbox, which could also be useful if the box must be left in an exposed or busy area of the house.

Used litter should be replaced on a regular basis. However, you can prolong the life of the litter by using a special scoop to clean it out after the cat has soiled in it. This will also help to eliminate unwelcome odors.

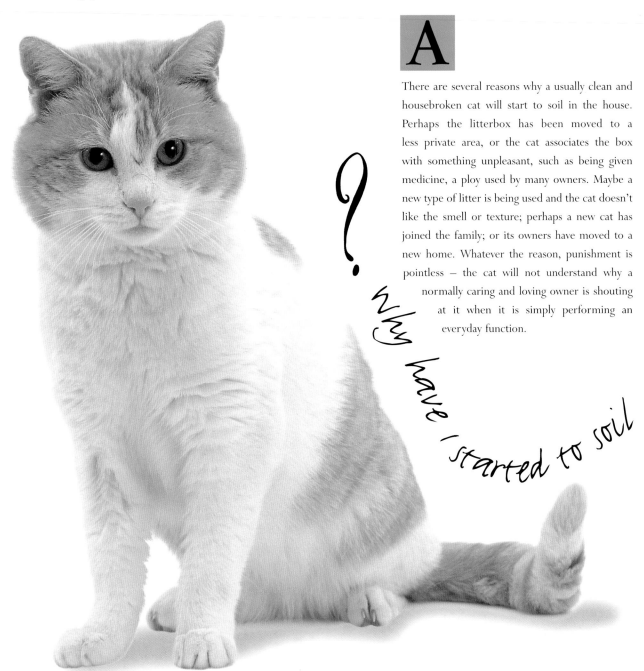

A

There are several reasons why a usually clean and housebroken cat will start to soil in the house. Perhaps the litterbox has been moved to a less private area, or the cat associates the box with something unpleasant, such as being given medicine, a ploy used by many owners. Maybe a new type of litter is being used and the cat doesn't like the smell or texture; perhaps a new cat has joined the family; or its owners have moved to a new home. Whatever the reason, punishment is pointless – the cat will not understand why a normally caring and loving owner is shouting at it when it is simply performing an everyday function.

? Why have I started to soil

? *So what should you do?*

Retraining is necessary, but before that it is essential to clean the area thoroughly to remove all smells, since the lingering odor encourages a cat to return to the same spot again and again. Avoid using bleach containing chlorine or ammonia, because these are compounds of the cat's urine, and will actually encourage the cat to continue soiling the same area. Swab the spot with white vinegar to hide any remaining smell. Then cover the area with cornflower or sodium bicarbonate, which can be vacuumed when dry, to help eliminate any lingering odor that only the cat can detect.

Trouble Spots

There are a few tricks to help deter a cat from soiling or spraying the same spot in the house.

Place the cat's food bowl on the spot. Cats dislike eating in the same place where they go to the bathroom.

Place a piece of polythene sheeting or aluminum foil on the spot because cats dislike the feel and sound of these materials.

? *What about cats spraying?*

Both male and female cats spray their territory, but this habit is especially noticeable in unneutered toms, and their urine is particularly pungent. Again, the area must be cleaned thoroughly. Whenever the cat looks about to start spraying, squirt its body (not its head) with water, or make a loud noise by throwing down a bunch of keys (near the cat, not at it).

If the cat persists in soiling the carpet, place a piece of carpet in a litterbox, and confine the cat and the litterbox to a room without a carpet, such as the bathroom. The cat will normally use the litterbox. Gradually cover the piece of carpet with litter, and remove it once the cat has relearned to use the litterbox.

Q. why do some cats urinate

A Many cats use a bathtub or sink as a toilet on occasion. This is probably because of a smell creeping up through the pipes that the cat associates with its own litterbox or toilet area, so it assumes this is an alternative toilet place. Or perhaps the bathtub or sink has just been cleaned and had ammonia poured down the drain. Ammonia contains chemicals that resemble the smells found in cats' urine, so this will also encourage the cat to relieve itself in the area. This behavior is usually intermittent, and once the smells vanish, the cat should resume using its regular toilet place.

If the cat insists on urinating in the tub or sink all the time, it may be that its litterbox is in an area that is unacceptable to the cat, and the relative privacy of the high-sided bathtub and the quiet of the bathroom may seem a preferable alternative. Check that the litterbox is privately located, kept clean, and located nowhere near the cat's food bowl. It may be worth investing in an enclosed litterbox. If the behavior persists, leave a little water in the tub or sink when it is not in use, and place the litterbox in the bathroom as a more comfortable alternative.

Attention! Attention!

Cats may be independent and able to look after themselves, but many revel in the pampering they get from their doting owners, and resent it when they are not the center of attention.

in the bathtub instead of in their litterbox

? Why *do some soil the bed?*

This behavior usually occurs when the cat is very stressed or nervous, because of a move, a change of owner, the arrival of a new baby, being left alone, or following an injury, for example. Initially, it may happen by accident. The cat may wake suddenly and feel isolated, or recall the situation that is causing it stress, and involuntarily soil the bed. From then on, the cat thinks of the bed as a toilet area. Another possible reason is if the cat suddenly feels abandoned by its owners, and tries to mix its scent with theirs in an effort to relieve its insecurity and strengthen the bond.

To prevent repeated incidents, the cat should be kept locked out of the bedroom for a while, until the association of bed and toilet has been forgotten. The cat should be shown more attention than usual, and reassured regularly. If it is unhappy at being left alone when the owner is away, it is kinder to put the cat in a kennel where it will feel more in control of its own space. Alternatively, it should be left in a smaller area of the house, and excluded from any room that it soils.

While it is recovering from an illness or an accident, you will probably give your cat more attention than usual, and lots of extra affection. When the cat is healthy again and life returns to normal, the cat may feign signs of the illness that brought it extra attention, such as limping or looking dejected, to regain some of that added affection.

Cats that have just been scolded often turn their backs on their irate owners, and refuse to answer to their names. This is not sulking, but an instinctive reaction to a threatening situation. The cat sees the human as a threat, and to break the tension, it turns its back, which is what it would do in a confrontation with another cat. Also, the owner may have been staring at it intently, which is very intimidating for a cat, so the cat turns away to break the hostile glare.

A If a cat is allowed into the yard to relieve itself, it can't be expected to use a certain spot only – and encouraging the cat to use a neighbor's yard isn't fair either. Training the cat to use a litterbox instead minimizes the risk of holes being dug in the yard, but any self-respecting cat will still mark its territory, which could damage plants. As a deterrent, surround prized plants with balloons that will burst if the cat tries to get through them, or cover the area with fine wire mesh, or prickly branches or leaves. Other suggestions are to cover the plants with a substance containing oil of citronella, or to bury mothballs near the surface. Alternatively, cover the surrounding earth with sharp gravel. However, make sure the cat is allowed some space of its own in the yard.

How do I know which part of the yard

? *Why* do I find some of your houseplants so tasty?

No one knows why for sure, but some cats do develop a taste for houseplants, especially if they don't have access to grass. But many houseplants, such as poinsettia and Christmas cherry, are poisonous for cats, so plant-eating should be discouraged immediately. Keep houseplants out of reach of cats. If this is not possible, surround the plants with jagged objects, or spray the leaves with diluted lemon juice. Alternatively, give the cat's body a squirt of water from a water pistol or squirt bottle every time it attempts to chew the plant.

? *Why* am I not allowed to chew electric cord?

Kittens and some cats, especially Oriental breeds, may chew wires through curiosity, boredom, or misplaced behavioral patterns. Whatever the reason, the practice could be fatal to the cat and cause fires. Try to keep cords hidden or inaccessible. If the cat starts to chew a cord, say a stern "No!" and place the cat firmly in another part of the room. Painting the wire with eucalyptus oil could also act as a deterrent.

to use as a bathroom ?

Plant Power

When you introduce a cat into the home, plants must be placed in safe locations to avoid damage to them and the cat. You can also provide the cat with a safe alternative.

Keep plants out of reach of the cat. A narrow ledge or a surface that is difficult to get to or balance on, such as the top of a television set, is a good choice.

Many cats like to eat grass, and if they do not have access to grass, they may chew houseplants. Grow a tub of grass, and keep it on the floor or somewhere accessible for the cat. Encourage the cat to eat the grass whenever it attempts to nibble the plants.

SPECIAL
FEATURE

Training a Kitten

Kittens are quick to learn and respond well to stroking and other signs of affection, but they can also be timid and feel vulnerable.

To achieve successful training and owner/kitten bonding, it is useful to follow some basic guidelines. First, give the kitten time to become familiar with its new home. Wherever the kitten has come from – a breeder, rescue organization, or a friend – it will feel nervous and isolated. Talk to it softly and stroke it gently. Let it become acquainted with your voice, touch, and smell. If it wants to sit under a table for the first day, let it; kittens are so inquisitive it won't be long before it is out exploring and looking for something to play with.

Early Days

In the first few days, keep the new kitten in one room or one part of the house, so that it gets used to its new surroundings and new owner. Try not to be too noisy – keep the television, radio, or CD player low, and don't have a riotous party to celebrate its arrival! Don't introduce the kitten to too many new people. If one or two of you are going to be its main owners, it needs to become accustomed to you and your voices. Too many strangers will confuse it.

Give the kitten a little food, and leave it to eat in peace. Cats don't like an audience

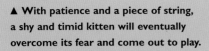

▲ With patience and a piece of string, a shy and timid kitten will eventually overcome its fear and come out to play.

▲ Show the kitten its food bowl and litterbox. The two should not be too close together.

when they're eating. Kittens between four and eight months old should be given small meals on a regular basis, about three to five times a day. Always be sure that there is fresh water available, but don't worry if it is ignored – the kitten is probably getting enough liquid from its solid food. As soon as the kitten has finished eating, place it gently in the litterbox, since the food will encourage it to go to the bathroom almost immediately after eating.

Making Friends

For the first day or so, try to keep other animals and young children away from the new arrival. Make sure that young children do not hit, grab, or chase the new kitten. If the kitten hides under a couch or behind the refrigerator, leave it alone. A disembodied hand waving in front of it is likely to get scratched or even bitten. Young children should sit on the floor when they are learning to hold a kitten, because they tend to drop the cat when it starts to wriggle or paddle with its claws.

When the kitten is to meet an established pet, such as a mature cat or dog, give the pair time and space to become acquainted, but always stay within earshot. If there is a scuffle, leave them to resolve it on their own, as long as no real damage is being caused. Restraining the animals will lead to further tension. Make sure your established pet has plenty of attention and cuddles to avoid jealousy. If the established pet is a smaller animal, such as a rabbit, guinea pig, or hamster, check that the kitten does not worry it or scare it, and don't ignore it in favor of the kitten.

Naming your Kitten

Kittens learn their names very quickly. Always use its name when playing with it or stroking it, and especially when giving it food. If it comes to you when its name is called, give it a small treat; this will encourage it to come when it is called at mealtimes. If you have decided to allow your cat to go out into the yard, only do so once the kitten has received its vaccinations and has grown accustomed to its new surroundings and new owners. For the first few days, only let it go out shortly before feeding time, and call to it frequently so that it associates the yard with you and the sound of your voice.

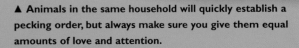

▲ **Animals in the same household will quickly establish a pecking order, but always make sure you give them equal amounts of love and attention.**

?why can't I scratch the furniture

A Scratching is instinctive behavior for cats; they do it to sharpen their claws and to mark out their territory. A cat is more likely to scratch the furniture if it doesn't go out, or if there is another cat in the house. Scratching furniture is something that should be stopped at the outset, because once a cat has started, it is difficult to train it to stop. A rolled-up newspaper tapped firmly next to the cat with a stern "No!" will help to prevent a habit from forming. Cats hate sudden loud noises. Alternatively, a squirt of water from a water pistol or squirt bottle aimed at the cat's body (not its head) should soon put it off. Avoid buying a couch covered in thick, woven material that a cat will find irresistible to scratch.

Sofa, So Good

There are a number of measures that can deter your cat from discovering the delights of scratching the furniture.

? Why can't I jump onto tables and kitchen surfaces?

Some cats like to observe their surroundings from the vantage point of a tabletop or other high surface, while others simply jump up to see what they can find to eat or play with. Some owners don't mind their cats jumping up onto furniture, but it should not be encouraged. Allowing a cat to jump onto kitchen surfaces can be dangerous. In kitchens where the top of the stove fits into the counter, a young or inexperienced cat may tread on a hot burner and burn its paws. Pots of hot water can be upturned, scalding the cat; or sharp objects might be pawed or sniffed as potential playthings, with nasty results. In addition, it is unhygienic to allow cats on a surface where food is prepared.

To stop a cat jumping up onto a table, simply say a stern "No!" and place the cat gently but firmly onto the floor. A cat will respond to the tone of a voice, and it will soon come to associate the "No!" with wrong behavior. If the cat is persistent, a sharp tap with a rolled-up newspaper on the surface next to the cat should soon stop it. Never hit a cat, and never sweep it off the surface onto the floor.

As an alternative to the sofa, buy a scratching post or make one from a sturdy log. A post with a perch for the cat to sit on might solve the tabletop problem, too!

Cats don't like smooth, shiny material. Fix a piece of material like this over the arms of the couch and chairs as a deterrent.

A Q. Why can't I scrounge a few tidbits from

While scrounging for food might look cute initially, the novelty soon wears off and develops into an intrusive and annoying habit – especially if there are some guests who don't think cats are the best thing in the whole world! Always feed the cat before guests arrive, so that it is not hungry when they are sitting down to eat. Don't allow guests to feed it from the table. A sharp "No!" in a scolding tone of voice should teach the cat not to beg for food. As a last resort, shut the cat out of the room until the meal is finished.

? Why do I run away when your friends visit?

Provided a cat has been handled with consistent gentleness since it was a kitten, and has not had any traumatic experiences with humans, there is no reason why it shouldn't welcome visitors to the house. Most confident cats enjoy meeting new people, with new smells and new bags to investigate. And everyone knows how a cat loves to head straight for the human who is allergic to it or doesn't like cats, so that it can sit on that person's lap and enjoy his or her discomfort! It is difficult to know why a normally friendly and sociable cat suddenly runs at the approach of strangers. Perhaps one guest was particularly noisy, or unknowingly frightened the cat.

your dinner guests ?

Meet the Guests

Retraining an adult cat is more difficult than training a kitten, but with patience it can be done. Reestablishing a cat's confidence in accepting visitors to the house takes time and should be done gently.

Never try to force a cat to be nice – it won't be! Holding a struggling cat to meet a guest will result in scratches all around and an even more nervous cat.

? *How do I cope with a young child?*

Most cats are surprisingly tolerant of young children, and put up with quite a lot of pulling and pushing unless they are being hurt. Kittens want to play, and in the excitement, might scratch or bite a youngster unintentionally. Always supervise toddlers and cats when they are together, and show the child how to stroke a cat gently. If the cat is elderly, or generally curmudgeonly and not child-friendly, keep it out of the room.

Confine the cat in the room where the guests are to be entertained. Make sure they ignore the cat at first, and it will probably sit under a table. At this stage, the cat just needs to become accustomed to their presence, and to realize that no harm is going to come to it.

As the cat becomes less nervous around guests, encourage them to approach the cat with a treat and allow the cat to take it from them. If they can, the guests should stroke the cat gently, but never attempt to pick it up or drag it out of its hiding place.

Do I have to wear a collar?

A

There are two main reasons for a cat to wear a collar: First, as a means of identification if the cat becomes lost or suffers an accident. Second, as a means of keeping fleas at bay. A collar with a bell can also be used to help deter bird-catching. It is best to accustom the cat to wearing a collar while it is still a kitten, because it may be harder to do so when the cat is older. Begin by fastening a collar loosely around the kitten's neck – the action of pulling a collar over its head may make it feel threatened and it will back away. Use a collar with an elasticized section, so that if the collar becomes caught, the kitten will not choke. Check that there is room to slip two fingers comfortably under the collar. Most kittens get used to a collar almost immediately, but keep an eye on the kitten to make sure that it is not distressed or irritated by the collar. If it is, remove the collar and replace it the next day until the kitten becomes accustomed to it. Flea collars are not suitable for kittens.

? *Can I be taken for a walk on a leash?*

It's not easy, but it can be done. Some breeds, such as Siamese and Burmese, are more amenable to leash-walking than other breeds, but most cats refuse point-blank. When putting a cat on a leash, always attach it to a harness rather than a collar, because many cats will be able to slip through a collar. Begin by putting the harness and leash on the cat and letting it drag the leash around at home. Then hold the other end, and let the cat roam where it wants to go. Gradually begin to guide the cat to go where the leash takes it. Don't attempt to take it for a walk outside until the cat is confident on the leash and you have control.

Cat in a Flap

For the independent cat, a cat door is a good idea if the owner is not always available to act as doorperson.

A simple cat door allows a cat to come and go as it pleases. Buy one with a lock if you don't want the cat to go out at night, and for security reasons. Be sure that the door is positioned at the right height for the cat, about 6in (15cm) from the floor. Partly lift the door and guide the cat through. Place some food on the other side to encourage the cat to go through if it is hesitant. Make sure that the door doesn't slam down behind it. Most cats learn how to use a cat door quickly and easily.

An electromagnetic cat door can only be opened and closed by a cat wearing the right magnet on its collar. This is useful to prevent strange cats from coming in and out, especially if the resident cat is unspayed.

What is a good diet to keep me healthy

How often should I be fed

Chicken, I love it! Why can't I have the bones as well

SPECIAL FEATURE: Weightwatching

What can I eat when I'm not well

Why do I scratch around my food bowl

Can I be a vegetarian

What is all the fuss about catnip

Why do I drink puddle water when fresh water is available

Feeding your Cat

A cat has a complex digestive system, which means that its diet needs to be carefully balanced. However, cats can often be fastidious eaters, so it is important that you understand what your cat needs to stay healthy, and how to put together a diet that will also keep it happy.

what is a good diet to keep me healthy

A If cats do not receive a well-balanced diet, it will show in their appearance and could lead to serious illnesses. A cat's diet should contain the same nutrients as a human's. They need protein for growth and tissue repair, essential fatty acids to keep their coats shiny, vitamin A for healthy eyes, calcium and vitamin D for strong bones and teeth, and carbohydrates for fiber and energy. They do not need vitamin B_{12}, and they make vitamins C and K within their body. Foods containing calcium are good for healthy teeth and bones. Dry food, cat chews, and bones exercise a cat's teeth and gums and help to get rid of tartar, but never give a cat bones that splinter. Uncooked limb bones are best.

? *What is a good diet for a kitten?*

Kittens start eating solid food when they are about four to five weeks old, though they may try some of their mother's food earlier than this. Introduce a kitten to weaning by offering it small semiliquid meals that it can lap, such as milk and cereal or finely ground cooked fish and chicken. Many excellent foods, both dry and canned, are produced specifically to meet the nutritional needs of growing kittens. Start serving these after the kitten has reached six weeks.

Cat Cuisine

Although commercial foods offer the ideal balance of nutrients and a complete diet, many owners like to feed their cat fresh foods. In such cases, care must be taken to ensure that the cat's diet remains nutritionally balanced.

? *Is commercial food best for me?*

Pet food manufacturers have devoted an enormous amount of research to cat food, and since it provides all the vitamins, minerals, and other nutrients required to keep a cat healthy, it can be used as a complete diet. Canned food contains a lot of moisture. Cats who eat only dry food should always have fresh water available; otherwise, bladder problems might occur. Cats do enjoy some variety in their diet. This can be achieved by feeding both dry and canned food in different flavors. Occasional treats, such as fresh meat and fish, will be much appreciated, but may lead to finicky eating habits. Do not serve dog food on a regular basis, because it does not contain the nutrients that cats require.

Fish, red meat, poultry, eggs, and cheese are good sources of protein. Don't give a cat raw egg whites, and not more than two eggs a week. Cheese can be served cooked or raw. Oily fish has the added benefit, in some cases, of helping the cat to get rid of furball.

Vegetables are good for cats, but they are unlikely to consider them a gastronomic treat! Add cooked leftover vegetables to the cat's regular food, but if the cat won't eat vegetables, it doesn't matter. If your cat likes fruit, treat it to an occasional slice or segment.

Starchy foods, such as rice and pasta, provide bulk and fiber, but they should not comprise more than a third of each meal.

A Kittens up to the age of five months should be fed four to five small meals a day. From five to twelve months, the number of meals can be reduced until the adult amount has been established. A healthy adult cat should have two meals a day, but tests have shown that cats generally prefer to eat little and often throughout the day. However, a cat is likely to adapt its feeding habits to suit the household routine, so there are no hard and fast rules about the amount of food or when to feed. Always be sure that food is fresh and protected from flies. Wet cat food quickly becomes stale and prone to bacteria when exposed. Usually the bowl should be emptied of old food, cleaned, and replenished every 24 hours. During hot weather, cat food should be stored in the refrigerator, but allow it to warm up a little before serving it to the cat. Cats prefer their food to be at body temperature, which would be the temperature of their natural prey. Feeding a cat tidbits between meals can result in finicky eating habits and obesity.

How often

should I be fed ?

Serving Suggestions

Although cats would prefer to eat their food off the floor, they are quite happy to eat from a bowl or plate, provided it suits their requirements. Always keep your cat's eating dishes and serving forks and spoons clean.

? How long can I go without eating?

Cats can survive without food for much longer than humans, and have been known to survive for weeks without food and water. However, this is an exception. While a cat can survive for long periods without food, lack of water leads to dehydration, which is usually fatal. Generally speaking, cats do not drink much, because they get most of their water from their food. Cats should never be left alone at home without access to food for longer than a day. Not only will the sudden "abandonment" and change in their feeding routine distress them, if they have access to a cat door, they may go off in search of food elsewhere, which could result in their getting involved in accidents or becoming lost.

Small plates make good serving dishes, but many cats will drag the food off the plate and eat it from the floor. Large plates are unsuitable, because they oblige the cat to stretch across to reach the food or to stand on the edge of the plate.

Glazed pottery bowls or plastic bowls made especially for cats are ideal serving dishes. Cats do not like to eat from a bowl that is too deep – they need to keep an eye on what is going on around them as they eat. A high rim could also touch the cat's neck and interfere with swallowing.

Automatic timed feeders help to keep food fresh and maintain a cat's feeding routine when the owner is away. They are only suitable if the cat is left for 24 hours at most. Any longer and the cat should be looked after by reliable neighbors or put in a kennel.

Chicken, I love it. – Why can't I have the

A

Since ancient Egyptian times, cats have caught and eaten birds, bones and all, in the wild, without causing themselves any harm. Wild cats need the calcium they get from the bones of their prey, and the exercise their teeth and gums get from eating the bones. Because the bones are small and uncooked, they do not seem to cause any problems. For domestic cats, however, cooked chicken bones and fish bones can create difficulties, and are best avoided to prevent any injury to the cat. Cooked chicken bones can splinter and pierce the gut, and bones can become trapped in the roof of the mouth or caught on a canine tooth, so that the cat finds it hard to dislodge them. If a cat really enjoys bones, it should be given uncooked limb bones, such as lamb or beef, or commercial dog bones. Alternatively, chewy treats may help to satisfy the cat's need to gnaw.

❓ *Liver, I love it! Why don't I have it more often?*

Liver is a prime source of vitamin A, and as such may be fed to a cat about once every 10 days or so. However, cats on a balanced diet do not require additional vitamin A, so feeding liver can result in nutritional imbalance and cause diarrhea. Excessive liver can result in a buildup of vitamin A in the cat's body, which causes severe physical ailments, such as joint pain, lameness, and loss of appetite. Bony outgrowths may also develop, which can cripple the cat and cause extreme pain. Keep liver as an occasional treat.

bones as well ❓

Feeding Fads

Some cats develop a fad for one particular food, but this is not to be encouraged, since it can lead to nutritional deficiencies and illnesses.

❓ *Fish, I love it! Why can't I have it every day?*

Any home-prepared diet that consists of only one type of food will result in deficiencies and an unhealthy buildup of one particular substance, which will have a detrimental effect on the cat's health. Too much fish, especially canned tuna fish, oily fish, and white fish, can result in the fat-storing cells just beneath the skin becoming inflamed. This causes pain, fever, lethargy, stiffness, and a dry, scaly coat. The condition is soon corrected with doses of vitamin E and the elimination of fish from the cat's diet, but it is best avoided in the first place.

If there is more than one cat in the household, you are unlikely to find a fussy eater. Always give each cat a separate bowl, and let them sort it out from there.

Gradually add different foods to a fussy cat's bowl, and reduce the amount of the preferred food.

SPECIAL
FEATURE

Weight-
watching

*Although a cat would never have the
chance to become even slightly overweight in the wild, obesity is a common
problem among domesticated cats.*

Many domesticated cats
lead fireside lives and are
overindulged by their
owners. An average cat
should weigh about 7–11
pounds (3–5 kg) – obviously
this will vary slightly with
different breeds. Although
being overweight does not
present the range of health
problems for a cat that it
does for humans and dogs,
the extra weight puts a
strain on the cat's heart,
liver, and joints, especially
in elderly cats, and a very
overweight cat will have a
shorter life expectancy.

Weighing your Cat

It is easy to see if a cat is
very overweight, but a
simple guide to
check if your
cat is getting
fat is the rib
test. If you
cannot feel each of

your cat's ribs without
pressing harder than
normal stroking, it is
probably overweight. If the
ribs feel pencil sharp,
however, your cat is
probably underweight.

Older cats, especially
females, develop loose flesh
that hangs down from the
stomach. This does not
necessarily mean that the
cat is fat, but give it the rib
test to be sure. A cat can
still be too thin, even
though it has this loose
flesh. Take it to the
veterinarian for a checkup
if in any doubt.

To weigh a small cat or
kitten, put it in a cardboard
box first. You can
then weigh

▲ **If your cat is a little overweight, adjust
the amount of food you give it or stop
feeding it treats.**

▼ **Stroke your cat along its
sides without squeezing. You
should be able to feel all its
ribs, but they should not be
sticking out.**

the empty box and figure out the difference. For a bigger or more uncooperative cat, hold the cat, weigh yourself and the cat together, then subtract your weight to arrive at the cat's weight. You may decide to put both of you on a diet!

Dieting

There are a number of medical reasons why a cat may be overweight, so take your cat to the veterinarian for a thorough checkup before embarking on a diet. If the reason is medical, the veterinarian can recommend the correct treatment. If not, it may be because you are overindulging the cat. Or it is lazy or elderly and not getting enough exercise. Or both. Perhaps it is eating with you and several of the neighbors as well. Whatever the reason, you will need to impose a strict regime of less food and more exercise for your cat.

If the cat is very overweight, the veterinarian should prescribe a corrective diet. In most cases, however, the cat will probably be just a little overweight, and you will know whether you have been feeding it too much. The average cat needs two meals a day, composed of roughly one can of ready-made food, that is, around 14½ ounces (420 g) of food per day. If your cat is having a can for breakfast, a can for dinner, and treats in between, cutbacks are called for. Don't leave food out all day, but feed your cat strictly two meals only, and cut out the treats. If this is already what you feed your cat, switch to another brand of food, because some manufacturers put more fiber and bulk in their foods than others. Or give the cat only half a can a day – it could be getting extras elsewhere.

It is essential that cats on a diet lose weight gradually. Crash dieting and sudden withdrawal of food can cause fatal liver disease in cats. Always conduct a cat's weight-loss diet under veterinary supervision.

Exercise

Make some time to play with your cat. Fifteen minutes a day playing with a small ball, some rolled-up paper, or a cork on a piece of string will lighten your cat's load and make you feel good as well. Leave some empty bags and open cardboard boxes around. Most cats will be tempted to explore these and will get some exercise in the process.

Remember, a fat cat is not a contented cat; it is a cat with a shorter life and a tendency to suffer from painful illnesses.

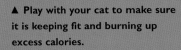

▲ **If your cat keeps wandering off and won't stay on the scales, place it in a cardbox box first.**

▲ **Play with your cat to make sure it is keeping fit and burning up excess calories.**

? Why *do I occasionally lose interest in my food?*

This usually happens after a certain food has caused a stomach upset, and the aversion to it is probably an instinctive reaction to prevent repeated illness. Another reason could be because the cat's food bowl has developed a buildup of odors, in which case invest in a new bowl. Sometimes, if the weather suddenly becomes very hot, the cat may not feel like eating, or, more likely, the heat is causing the food to smell bad. Or maybe the bowl has changed position – cats do not like to eat in a bright, busy, noisy area. Cats can go for a long time without eating, but check that the cat is drinking more to compensate for the lack of moisture it would normally get from its food. If the cat is trying to eat but having difficulty, there may be something stuck in its throat or teeth, and it should be taken to the veterinarian immediately.

A

This is not the cat's way of saying the cook should be fired, but rather an instinctive action to cover up the food and save it for another time. In the wild, the cat would probably eat all of its prey at one sitting, but if it did not, it would cover it with leaves or earth for when it was next hungry.

Q. Why do I scratch around my

food bowl

Drag Act

Most cats, at one time or another, drag their food off the dish and eat it from the floor. This could be for the reasons already outlined – lingering odors that repel the cat and encourage it to take its food elsewhere.

Cats like a bowl or plate to be wider than their whiskers, otherwise they may drag the food outside it.

If the meal contains a large piece of meat or a safe bone, this will resemble prey caught in the wild, and the cat may instinctively drag it away as it would in the wild. Put the food back in the bowl and say "No!" in a firm voice. Or feed the cat wet food that is impossible to drag out.

A

A sick cat will probably not feel like eating. Cats can survive for several days without food, but it is essential that they do not dehydrate, so the cat should be fed nourishing liquid food, such as beef tea or warm water with honey or glucose, in small quantities. Invalid foods, such as hydrolyzed protein (available from a veterinarian or pet store), are worth trying. Spoonfeed the cat if necessary. Syringe feeding may become necessary if the cat is too weak to eat, but keep force-feeding to a minimum, and never give food or liquid of any kind to an unconscious animal, which can easily choke. When the cat is getting better, build up its strength with small, regular meals. It is important to get the cat eating normally again as soon as possible, so tempt it with its favorite tidbits. However, make sure its diet remains nutritious.

?what can I eat when

Tempting Tricks

A cat that has lost interest in food may need to have its appetite restored slowly and gently. Cats are attracted to food through smell, so if the cat has a reduced sense of smell due to respiratory problems, it will need to be tempted with strong-smelling foods.

I'm not well?

Pungent foods, such as mackerel, sardines, and tuna, may tempt your cat's tastebuds. Alternatively, add beef stock or yeast extract to the cat's normal food. If the cat has respiratory problems, keep its nose clean. A nasal spray may help the cat to regain its sense of smell, and thus its appetite.

Smear a small piece of food on the cat's nose, which it should lick off. This may help to kickstart the cat's appetite.

? *Which is best for me, raw or cooked meat and fish?*

For cats fed on a diet of fresh food, it is generally best to serve cooked meat, because cooking kills germs and toxins, including the parasite that causes toxoplasmosis – a disease that can be passed to humans. Fish should also be cooked. Raw fish, such as herring and carp, contains high levels of the enzyme thiamine, which destroys the vitamin B_1 in other foods in the diet, resulting in a deficiency. To avoid this, and to kill any germs and toxic substances that are present in fish due to pollution, always feed the cat fish that has been lightly cooked.

If your cat is persistently refusing food, roll some food into a soft ball, about the size of a pea. Feed this to the cat as you would a pill. Do not force it unnecessarily, and take care that the cat doesn't choke.

Can I be a vegetarian?

A

No. Cats must have a regular amount of meat protein in their diet to remain healthy. An adult cat requires twice as much protein as a dog for body maintenance. Proteins are made up of amino acids, which are essential for the cat's proper growth and optimum health. Some of these amino acids can be obtained from non-meat sources, such as eggs and cereals, but some are only available from meat. One amino acid, taurine, is essential to prevent blindness and certain heart diseases. Most mammals can make taurine from other amino acids, but a cat cannot, so it needs a regular source of taurine from meat.

A cat's digestive system cannot manufacture linoleic acid from its food, and this is obtained from the fat found in meat. Linoleic acid is essential in making new blood cells, and helps with a number of essential body functions, such as blood clotting and reproduction. Finally, cats cannot make vitamin A from plant sources, only from animal tissue, and vitamin A is essential for normal, healthy bodily functions. Feeding cats a premium, commercial diet will ensure they receive all the protein and other nutrients they need.

? *Do I need vitamin and mineral supplements?*

If a cat is eating a good, balanced diet, including a high percentage of reputable commercial cat food, then no. But if the cat is on a largely meat-only diet, it may need additional calcium, phosphorus, and vitamin B, which can be provided by adding sterilized bone meal or some commercial alternative to the cat's meat. However, too much can be dangerous, so always follow the manufacturer's recommendations.

? *Are there natural supplements I can take?*

For a more natural approach, try parsley, which is full of calcium, phosphorus, iron, and vitamins A, B, C, and E. Alfalfa is a good general tonic, especially for a recuperating cat; it stimulates appetite and digestion, thus improving weight gain and the overall condition of the cat. Half a teaspoonful of powdered alfalfa should be mixed with the cat's food each day. Additional supplements may be useful for sick or pregnant cats, and a veterinarian can advise on these.

Little Extras

However varied your cat's diet is, it will still go in search of a little extra something.

Most cats eat grass at some time or other. Grass is a natural emetic, and it could help the cat to vomit and so get rid of furball. It could also be a way of obtaining more vitamin B, often missing in a mainly meat diet, or it could provide fiber to help with constipation. Eating grass can only harm a cat if the grass has been recently sprayed with herbicide or insecticide.

Nearly all cats that are allowed outdoors will hunt and kill birds or small animals at one time or another, no matter how well fed they are. The need to hunt is a deep and powerful instinct, and has to be accepted. There is no point in scolding a cat that has brought home a bird, because for the cat this is perfectly natural behavior.

A

The herb catnip is to some cats what a glass of wine is to humans. It intoxicates them. They feel silly and they want to play with the catnip, rubbing against it, pawing it, throwing it in the air, and catching it. It is thought that catnip excites cats because it contains a chemical that resembles the smell of a substance secreted by an unspayed female, and toms are usually more affected by catnip than neutered males and females. Another herb, valerian, has a similar effect. Both are completely harmless to the cat.

What is all the fuss about catnip?

? Why would I suddenly develop odd eating habits?

Cats can suddenly develop a taste for many nonfood items, but the most common are wool and fabric. Wool-sucking occurs especially in orphaned or undernourished cats, and those that have been weaned too early. It is also a response to stress. The wool is a substitute for the mother's nipple, and as the cat sucks the wool, it will also knead with its paws and purr, reenacting the behavior of a kitten suckling. It is thought that the smell of lanolin in the wool reminds the cat of its mother. This behavior often fades away as the cat gets older, but it can continue for a lifetime.

It is a dangerous habit, because pieces of fabric can be ingested and cause an obstruction in the cat's stomach, which has to be surgically removed. Often cats become so engrossed in this behavior that the usual "punishments" of making a loud noise or saying a firm "No!" are ignored. Taste deterrents, such as eucalyptus or menthol, sprayed on pieces of old clothing that are left in a prominent position have been successful in curbing this, but in some cats it is a deep compulsion. Apart from fabric, cats have been known to chew rubber, such as the seal of a refrigerator and electric cords, which is obviously dangerous to both cat and owner. This nonnutritional eating behavior is known as *pica*.

Easy Pickings

Today's domestic cat usually has to do little more than turn up at a certain time each day to find its food ready and waiting, cut into easy-to-swallow chunks – a far cry from the stalk, chase, pounce, and kill routine required in the wild.

Sometimes pica is due to a lack of outlets for the cat's normal feline behavior, such as hunting for its own food. Try giving the cat tougher chunks of meat, so that it feels it is wrestling with a huge wildebeest. Or hide its food in different parts of the house, or cover the bowl with paper or a twig, so that it has to work for its supper.

One reason cats sometimes scavenge food is because they following age-old instincts to hunt the food for themselves. They will even hunt insects and spiders.

Giving the cat smaller meals on a regular basis, and bulking out its food with fiber, might also help to keep it feeling full.

why do I drink puddle water when fresh wate

A Cats can survive for quite a while without food, but water is essential. A bowl of clean, fresh water should always be available, especially for a cat on a dry diet. Cats get a lot of their moisture through their food, and a cat being fed a dry diet needs up to seven times as much water as one on a wet diet. The cat often refuses to drink the fresh water, choosing instead dirty puddle water.

It may be that the fresh water is too cold – cats like their food and drink at body temperature – or that it is sensitive to the chemicals used to process the domestic water supply. Sometimes a bowl of water will be drunk after a couple of days, when the chemicals have evaporated. Always check that both food and water bowls are well rinsed of all detergents, since the smell from these will repel a cat. This is particularly important with drinking bowls, as the combined odor of water chemicals and detergent, and the lack of food smells to help counteract it, will send the cat off on its own water hunt.

is available

A Drink Problem

One explanation why cats seem to prefer drinking from puddles, ponds, bathtubs, and even toilets is that these are the domestic cat's equivalent to the watering hole. In its wild state, after eating, a cat looks for a watering hole to quench its thirst, and the small bowl in the kitchen corner is just no substitute.

? *Should I have milk instead of water?*

No. Water is the essential liquid for a cat. Milk can be offered as an additional treat, but it should not be used as a substitute for water. In many adult cats, cow's milk causes severe diarrhea, which can be life-threatening, since it causes dehydration. Sometimes goat's milk can be drunk instead, but as milk is not essential, it is probably best avoided altogether.

Try putting your cat's water in a bigger container, such as the base of a large flowerpot.

If you spot a cat tapping the surface of the water before drinking, this is to create a vibration, so that it can gauge how far away the water is. That way, it avoids getting its nose wet!

? *Is water ever bad for me?*

The only time a cat should not be allowed to drink water is when it is vomiting. Vomiting will make the cat thirsty and it will want to drink, but this will only cause it to vomit more, resulting in dehydration. After vomiting, all food and liquids should be stopped for about two hours. After this time, begin to give the cat small amounts of water. If the cat does not vomit again, give it some liquid at hourly intervals. If the cat does vomit again, wait for at least eight hours before giving it any more liquid. If the cat continues to vomit, consult a veterinarian immediately.

How would you choose
a veterinarian for me

What is my
third eyelid

How should you
look after me if
I'm sick

Can I pass on
diseases to
humans

How would you care for
me in an emergency

SPECIAL
FEATURE:
A safe home

Why do I keep
scratching myself

Why do I spend
so much time
cleaning

What grooming
would I need if
I had long hair

Why is it important
to neuter male cats

Why do I need
help looking
after my teeth

How do you know
when a female is
ready to mate

What will I be
like when I'm old

Caring for your Cat

Cats are very good at looking after themselves, but their natural curiosity and unavoidable illnesses require their owners to have a certain amount of first-aid and medical knowledge. Safety in the home, resuscitation techniques, the early signs of illness, and neutering are just a few of the subjects that a loving cat owner needs to know about.

How would you choose a veterinarian for me

A Choosing a veterinarian to care for a cat is almost as important as choosing a doctor or dentist for a human. Ask for recommendations from other pet owners and ask about their services, their fees, consulting hours, and emergency capabilities. Visit the veterinarian, and watch how he or she handles the cat. Treatment can be very expensive, and the veterinarian can advise on health insurance for the cat. Take the cat to the veterinarian for an annual checkup and vaccinations. If the cat looks sick, stops eating, or appears to have trouble emptying its bladder or bowels, take it to the veterinarian immediately.

? *Why* are you so interested in my bathroom habits?

When a cat is sick, any inconsistencies in its feces and urine can help the veterinarian to make a swift diagnosis. Discreetly noting the cat's posture when it goes to the bathroom can provide an early warning sign of any bowel or bladder problems. A healthy cat will urinate quickly and without strain or pain, and its posture should be relaxed. If the cat does not pass urine or feces, take it to the veterinarian. If the cat appears to be straining or tense, and holds its head down or cries out, there could be a serious problem, and the cat should be taken to the veterinarian.

? *Must* I have vaccinations every year?

Yes, for feline infectious enteritis (FIE) and upper respiratory illness (sometimes known as cat flu). FIE is a highly contagious and fatal virus that attacks the cat's digestive system. The virus acts so quickly that often symptoms are not recognized until it is too late. Upper respiratory illness is a general term used for a number of different viruses that have very similar symptoms, including loss of appetite, sneezing, and conjunctivitis. If neglected, it can develop into pneumonia, which can be fatal. All kittens should be vaccinated against both FIE and upper respiratory illness at about eight weeks of age, and not allowed to leave the house or mix with other cats until then. After that, the vaccinations should be given regularly every year. Cats can also be vaccinated against a number of other viruses, such as the feline leukemia virus. Vaccinations are especially important if the cat goes outdoors, spends time in a kennel, or lives with other cats.

Lost and Found

If your cat is in an accident or gets lost, it is important that anyone who finds it is able to contact you.

Another method is to have the cat microchipped. A tiny microchip containing a pin number is injected under the skin in the cat's neck. If whoever finds the cat takes it to a veterinarian with the necessary facilities, the veterinarian will scan the cat and check the pin number on a database that contains the details of the cat's owners.

A collar with a tag giving the cat's name and telephone number is the easiest way of identifying a cat. Check regularly to make sure the cat is still wearing the collar, however, as some cats regularly slip out of their collars, or get them caught on branches.

? *Is the third eyelid always a sign of illness?*

The nictitating membrane can become visible in perfectly healthy cats for no apparent reason, and in some cats a small corner of the third eyelid may be seen all the time.

what is my third eyelid ?

A

The third eyelid – sometimes known as the haw – is on the inside corner of the cat's eye. This is the nictitating (or blinking) membrane, which helps to protect the cat's eyes. If the cat is subject to too much bright light, the nictitating membrane partially covers the eye to filter the dazzle. It also cleans the surface of the eye, and protects it from dirt and dust. Sometimes, a small grass seed or piece of grit may get trapped under it, and this may need to be removed under anesthetic. If the cat's eye is weeping or the cat keeps pawing its face, or if only one nictitating membrane can be seen, consult your veterinarian.

In many cases, the haw only becomes visible when the cat is debilitated or has a virus, or is recuperating from an illness. In these circumstances, the fat stored around the eyes to help cushion them from blows is broken down to provide essential energy for the cat. The eyes sink back and become partially covered by the nictitating membrane. It looks alarming, but can be a useful warning sign of illness. If it remains visible for more than a day or two, take the cat to the veterinarian.

? *Should I have a wet nose?*

There are many everyday signs that indicate whether a cat is ailing or not, and a wet nose is one of them. A healthy cat will have a moist nose, but it should not be runny. The cat should be generally alert and active, and eat and drink normally. If the cat starts to vomit, to cough and sneeze, and to paw at its eyes or ears or shake its head, it should visit the veterinarian.

Checkup

If a cat appears listless and lacks interest in food, or the nictitating membrane is visible, or the coat looks coarse and dull, the cat may be coming down with an illness. The following procedures can help you decide whether or not to seek veterinary advice. If there is any doubt, however, it is always better to consult a veterinarian than to wait until it is too late, because cats can deteriorate very quickly.

Check the cat's teeth and gums. Its teeth should be white, and its gums and palate pink. If the teeth or gums are yellow, or the cat has particularly bad breath, seek the advice of a veterinarian.

To take a cat's pulse, place the cat on a tabletop. Try to keep the cat calm by being gentle and unhurried, and talking to it soothingly. Feel along the inside of one of its back legs, high up where the leg meets the body in the groin area. A healthy cat will have a pulse of around 120 beats per minute.

To take a cat's temperature, you will probably need a helper. Use a clinical stubby-ended glass thermometer, and flick it a couple of times to make sure the mercury is at the bulb end. Smear it with petroleum jelly, lift the cat's tail, and gently insert the thermometer into the cat's anus until about 1in (2.5cm) of it is inside the cat. Angle the thermometer upward slightly, so that it touches the wall of the rectum. Hold it in position for about a minute, take it out, wipe it, and read the figure. A healthy cat will have a temperature of 100–101 °F (38–39 °C).

How should you look after me if i'm sick?

A sick cat is a pitiful sight, and while the urge to pick it up and cuddle it may be overwhelming, don't. Sick and recuperating cats need and want to be left in peace, with the minimum amount of fuss. Find a quiet spot in the house that is safe, warm, and free from drafts. Make a bed of towels or sheets, or the cat's favorite blanket, and leave the cat alone. If the cat decides to find its own place to recover, under the bed or behind the couch, let it be. If the cat is very sick, be prepared to change soiled bedding and groom it regularly. Place a litterbox nearby, but not next to the food bowl.

? *Will I have to take any medicine?*

It is always best to consult a qualified veterinarian if a cat is sick, and tablets or liquid medicine may be prescribed. Always follow the veterinarian's instructions for the cat's medicine carefully, and complete the treatment as directed, even if the cat appears to be fully recovered. When giving medicine to a cat, be gentle but firm. Talk to it soothingly, and have someone to assist if possible. Try to make sure that the medicine is given successfully the first time, or the cat will become anxious and fidgety. Give the medicine while the cat is sitting or standing if it is not too ill. If the cat is really aggressive, wrap it in a towel.

A Helping Hand

Giving a cat medicine can be tricky, particularly once the cat is on the road to recovery and has regained some of its vitality.

To give a cat pills, grasp the cat's head from above, so that your forefinger and thumb are at the corners of its mouth. Tip the head back slightly, and gently press the forefinger and thumb in to force open the cat's mouth. Push the pill as far back on the cat's tongue as you can. Quickly close the cat's mouth and hold it closed, still with the head tipped back if possible.

Stroke the cat's throat in a downward direction to encourage swallowing. Keep the cat's mouth closed until it licks its nose, which indicates that the pill has been swallowed – many a cat has learned to pretend to swallow and then to spit the pill out later. Never crush a pill and sprinkle it onto the cat's tongue, because many pills have a bitter and unpleasant taste.

The easiest way to feed a cat liquid medicine is with a syringe from the veterinarian or pet store. Fill the syringe as necessary. Hold the cat's head gently but firmly, insert the syringe at the side of the cat's mouth, and squirt in a little at a time, so that the cat does not choke. Hold the cat's mouth shut afterwards.

can I pass on

A

Diseases passed from animals to humans are termed zoonoses. The most notorious of these is rabies, which can be passed on by a number of different types of animal. But a human is more likely to catch rabies from a wild animal than from a pet. Humans are at minimum risk from cats, but there are a few infections and viruses that can be passed on.

Toxoplasmosis is a parasite that cats pick up from raw meat, and which can then be passed to humans, usually through the cat's feces. This disease can be serious in a child or a pregnant woman. High standards of hygiene should be maintained, including wearing gloves when gardening and cleaning litterboxes, and insisting that children wash their hands thoroughly after playing in the park or yard.

Ringworm, fleas, lice, and fur mites can also sometimes be passed to humans from cats. They cause skin reactions, such as blotches and itching, but can be easily treated. It is preferable, however, to keep the cat free of these parasites to create a healthier home environment for everyone. Scratches and bites from a cat can result in infections, and should be cleaned well with antiseptic. However, if a cat is handled with care and respect, it shouldn't bite or scratch, unless it is ill or in pain.

Viruses such as feline leukemia and feline AIDS cannot be caught by humans, even if bitten by an infected cat.

diseases to humans

? **Can** *humans pass on diseases to cats?*

No human diseases can be transmitted to cats, but humans can carry the cat virus feline enteritis on their hands or clothes, and pass it on to another cat. That is why it is so important to keep the cat's vaccinations current.

Reckless Lifestyle

A cat's life isn't always a bowl of cream. Sometimes its owners have lifestyles and habits that a cat would rather live without.

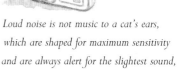

Loud noise is not music to a cat's ears, which are shaped for maximum sensitivity and are always alert for the slightest sound, even when the cat is asleep. Humans can hear lower frequencies than a cat, but a cat can hear a much higher range of sounds. Cats don't like loudness, and although there is no evidence to show that powerful noise can cause cats harm, if they could turn it down, they probably would.

Cats have an acute sense of smell, and they don't like the odor of cigarette smoke. Many cats will leave a room the minute a cigarette is lit, but most learn to tolerate it. Passive smoking will not cause cancer in a cat, but if the cat is prone to asthma, it can provoke an attack or make the asthma worse. If a cat has breathing difficulties or chest problems, such as feline bronchitis, being subjected to cigarette smoke will make them worse.

There is nothing in alcohol that would appeal to a cat, and generally cats won't touch a drop. Some cats do become addicted to drink, however, with the same disastrous results as in humans. They become confused and disoriented, and can suffer serious and fatal liver disease from their alcohol consumption.

How would you

A

If a cat has been injured, it is important to take it to a veterinarian as soon as possible. However, some immediate treatment on the spot can help to alleviate the cat's suffering, and may mean the difference between life and death.

If the cat is unconscious, turn it gently onto its side, but do not leave an unconscious cat on the same side for more than five to ten minutes. It should then be turned onto the other side. Do not move the cat unless it is in danger – in the middle of the highway, for example. Its head should point downhill, to aid the drainage of fluids and vomitus from the mouth. To move the cat,

slip a sheet or coat underneath it, and use it like a hammock. If the cat is in distress and lashing out, wrap it in a blanket or towel and place it in a basket or box. Support the basket or box underneath to keep it as steady as possible. If the cat is unconscious, open its mouth and pull the tongue forward. Remove any foreign body, using a pair of tweezers if necessary, and clear the mouth of any mucus with a cotton ball or an old, clean cloth. If the cat feels cold and its breathing and pulse are rapid, it may be in shock. In that case, wrap it in a warm blanket or towel, making sure its breathing is not restricted, or keep it warm with a hot water bottle wrapped in cloth. If the cat has an injured limb, lift it gently in a blanket or towel, with the injured limb uppermost, and take it to the veterinarian. Do not attempt to make a splint or treat it in any way.

? *What would you do if I swallowed some poison?*

Cats usually vomit readily to rid themselves of poison. However, if there are signs of poisoning – vomiting, paralysis, diarrhea, foaming at the mouth, and convulsions – contact a veterinarian immediately. Vomiting should not be induced unless advised by the veterinarian.

? *What would you do if I were drowning?*

Most cats are good swimmers, but if a cat does begin to drown, take it out of the water and dry it quickly with a towel. Grip its hind legs firmly with one hand, and swing the cat vigorously but smoothly downward to remove water from its lungs. Keep the cat warm and use a resuscitation technique if necessary.

care for me in an emergency

Resuscitation Techniques

? *What would you do if I were scalded?*

Drench the scald or burn in cold water from a cloth or cup. Apply an ice pack or a freezer bag, wrapped in a clean cloth, to the burn. Petroleum jelly can be gently rubbed into the scalded area. The wound should not be covered or smeared with butter or skin cream. Consult a veterinarian immediately, because the true extent of a burn often does not become apparent for several days.

If there is no detectable heartbeat or breathing, mastering these techniques could save a cat's life.

Lay the cat on its side and place a hand between its front legs, with the thumb on one side of the ribs and the fingers the other side. Squeeze the thumb and fingers together, compressing the rib cage and hence the heart. Stop pressing to allow the lungs to refill, then repeat the press/release rhythm every five seconds.

For mouth-to-mouth resuscitation, hold the unconscious cat's head in an upright position. Breathe into the cat's nostrils for two or three seconds to inflate the lungs. You will see the chest moving. Pause for a couple of seconds, rest, and repeat.

SPECIAL FEATURE

A Safe Home

Home should be a place of comfort and security, yet for a cat the human environment can be a dangerous place, full of unexpected hazards.

Inside the Home

Good training, such as not allowing the cat to jump up on work surfaces, will help to keep a cat safe, but cats are curious creatures, and might soon use up their nine lives if you do not take precautions to keep your home as safe as possible.

The kitchen is the most hazardous room in the home. Avoid leaving sharp objects lying around, and never leave cooking pans unattended. The cord of a hot iron can easily be pulled, with nasty results for the cat. Cats love to explore, and an open door is irresistible for some cats. Keep the doors of washing machines and driers closed, or check carefully before switching them on.

Any food left out will almost certainly be viewed as fair game, and it may contain bones that could injure the cat. Garbage pails should be kept covered, since a curious cat could get trapped in one, or rob it of an item that is harmful. If you are busy preparing a meal, it is best to keep the cat out of the kitchen

altogether, since it is bound to get under your feet, which could result in an accident.

In the kitchen and bathroom, beware of leaving out

▲ Cats that are allowed outside are subject to many dangers, and their inquisitive nature can lead them to explore the most inaccessible of places.

▼ Cats are playful, so a hanging electric cord will be virtually impossible for them to ignore – with potentially lethal results.

disinfectants, bleach, and detergents that can be overturned and the contents explored, causing possibly fatal poisoning. Aspirin is especially poisonous for a cat, and should be kept shut away.

Throughout the house, try to tuck away trailing electric cords. If you have an open fireplace, put a guard in front to prevent the cat from exploring the chimney, and possibly getting stuck in it. And, of course, a guard should always be used when the fire is burning. Don't leave plastic bags lying around — an inquisitive cat could get its head stuck and suffocate. If you have any houseplants that are poisonous to cats, such as

philodendrons, dumb cane, ivy, elephant's ears (caladiums), poinsettias, Christmas cherry, and oleander, give them to a cat-less friend or put them out of the cat's reach. If in doubt about a plant, consult your veterinarian.

In the Yard

The yard is another area of hidden dangers. Plants that are toxic to cats include azaleas, mistletoe, sweet pea, clematis, delphinium, laurel, rhododendron, lupines, and Christmas rose. A cat is unlikely to eat garden plants, but it is worth keeping an eye open just in case.

Cats can easily get shut in sheds and garages, or become trapped in old refrigerators or freezers that have been relegated to the garage, so keep doors shut. Insecticides and pesticides, slug and snail pellets, turpentine, cans of paint, oil, and antifreeze should all be tightly shut and kept out of the cat's reach.

If you see any signs of poisoning in your cat, such as twitching, muscle spasms, drooling, convulsions, foaming at the mouth, diarrhea, vomiting, staggering, impaired coordination, and lack of balance, take the cat to a veterinarian immediately, because all poisons strike quickly and are lethal.

▶ **Poisonous houseplants include (clockwise from bottom left): caladiums, ivy, poinsettias, dumb cane, and philodendrons.**

▲ **Poisonous outdoor plants include (clockwise from bottom left): lupines, clematis, sweet peas, delphiniums, and rhododendrons (center).**

A

Scratching is usually caused by fleas. They should be treated as soon as possible, because fleas can seriously affect a cat's health. Sprays and flea powders are effective, but can be difficult to apply. They also wash out in the rain and must be reapplied on a regular basis. Always follow the label recommendations carefully, and do not use these products on kittens. Fleas and flea eggs live in carpets, furniture, and particularly in the cat's bedding, so these areas must be treated also.

A country cat may have ticks or mites. These little arachnids burrow into the skin and drink the cat's blood. Ticks should never be pulled out without first killing them with alcohol, because their mouth parts may be left in the cat's body and cause an abscess. Treatments are available from pet stores, or you can consult a veterinarian. If a cat is scratching or biting a particular part of its body regularly, such as its ears or paws, it may have something stuck there. Examine the area gently, looking for any signs of swelling and tenderness. If in doubt, or if there is a foreign object that needs to be removed, consult with your veterinarian immediately.

Why do I keep scratching myself

? *Why do you worm me?*

There are four common worms that can infect a cat: roundworms, hookworms, whipworms, and tapeworms. If the worms are not eradicated early, they can cause serious problems, especially in kittens and young cats. The first signs of worms include an increase in the cat's appetite and a general loss of condition. Check the cat's anus for bits of tapeworm, which look like long grains of rice. If there is a possibility that the cat has worms, take it to the veterinarian; the most thorough check for worms is by laboratory examination of the feces. Most kittens acquire worms from their mothers, so they should be routinely wormed from four to twelve weeks of age under veterinary supervision.

? *When is a worm not a worm?*

When it is ringworm, which is a fungus. This contagious and unsightly skin complaint can also cause itching. Ringworm results in bald patches. Take the cat to the veterinarian for treatment. Humans can catch ringworm (it produces a circular skin rash that is easily treated), so the cat should be taken to the veterinarian quickly.

Mobile Homes

Most cats will be a home to fleas at some time or other, and the fleas should be eradicated immediately. Always select a treatment that was produced especially for cats. Many dog treatments contain chemicals that are dangerous for cats. If you have any doubts, consult a veterinarian.

Brushes with hollow spikes filled with flea powder allow the powder to be brushed easily through the cat's fur. Regular combing with a special flea comb can also keep fleas at bay. When using a flea comb, keep a bowl of water nearby in which to drown the fleas, or throw them into a fire. Fleas are almost impossible to squash, even with long, sharp fingernails.

The chemicals used in standard flea collars irritate some cats, causing skin problems, dizziness, and headaches. If you try a flea collar, choose one that is expandable, and check the fit regularly — you should be able to slide two fingers under the collar. Collars can cause injury or even death if they are caught on bushes or a tree branch.

Many high-tech products have been developed to help get rid of fleas. These range from tablets and injections to ultrasonic devices and pads soaked in flea pheromones (natural attractive secretions). Your veterinarian can advise the best treatment for your cat.

? Why do I spend so much time cleaning

A Cats are fastidious creatures and like to stay clean. Keeping its fur in tiptop condition is essential for a cat's well-being. Cats lick their fur to rid it of dirt, to strengthen their own smell if they have been handled, and to keep their coat waterproof. Repeated licking smooths the fur, and smooth fur provides better protection against the cold. Cleaning is also a displacement activity: when faced with an unsettling situation, a cat will start to lick its paws or wash its face, to avoid having to react immediately to the situation and to allow itself time to consider its next move.

? Why do I wash so thoroughly when I've just been stroked?

While most cats love a cuddle and stroke, it means their fur becomes impregnated with the human scent, weakening the cat's own smell. Also, their fur will be ruffled. A good lick replaces their own scent and smooths their fur.

From Top to Bottom

Cats spend a great deal of time cleaning themselves, and can twist themselves into all sorts of contortions to reach those difficult-to-get-to places.

Why do I lick myself when the weather is hot?

Cats do not have pores or sweat glands, so when it is hot they must find another way to keep cool. They lick themselves repeatedly, leaving a layer of saliva along their fur. This acts like human sweat. As the saliva dries and evaporates, it lifts heat from the cat's skin.

Why do I tug at my fur when cleaning myself?

This is an important part of the grooming process. The tugging stimulates glands in the skin. When these glands are stimulated, a secretion is released that helps to keep the cat's coat waterproof.

A cat's cleaning routine follows a set pattern, starting from the head, working along the front legs and shoulders, then down the flanks to the genitals and hind legs, and ending with its tail, from base to tip.

Cats can contort themselves to reach nearly every part of their body for cleaning. The only areas they can't reach, either with tongue or paw, is between their shoulderblades.

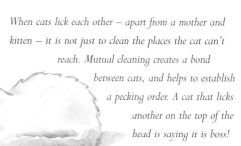

When cats lick each other – apart from a mother and kitten – it is not just to clean the places the cat can't reach. Mutual cleaning creates a bond between cats, and helps to establish a pecking order. A cat that licks another on the top of the head is saying it is boss!

A

Q. what grooming would I need if

Most cats with long hair are Persians, which have exceptionally thick coats, round bodies, a short nose, and round eyes. Persians are bred in a variety of different colors, from the odd-eyed white, with one amber and one blue eye, to the dramatic-looking pure black longhair, with dark orange or copper eyes. Non-Persian longhairs include the Balinese, Ragdoll, Angora, Turkish Van, and Maine Coon. Longhairs have extremely dense coats and shed throughout the year, so it is essential to groom them every day. If not, the fur will become matted, which is painful for the cat, and it will need to be cut by a veterinarian. Longhairs are also more likely to develop serious furballs, which might have to be surgically removed. Loose hairs can get caught around the cat's lower canine teeth, and build up into a thick rope of hair that bites into the gums, causing inflammation.

Grooming with a special wide-toothed comb and a bristle brush once a day will help to prevent all this. It will keep the coat looking smooth and shiny, and tone up the cat's circulation and muscles — and possibly the owner's also! Sprinkle tangles with talcum powder, and gently tease out the knots by hand — don't tug with a comb or brush, because this is painful. Sprinkling on a little talcum powder before grooming will also help to clean the fur if it is very dirty.

had long hair ?

? What grooming would I need if I had short hair?

Shorthaired cats require less grooming than longhairs. However, a regular brush will help to keep the cat's coat clean and shiny, and reduce the development of furballs. This is especially important when the cat is shedding.

? Do hairless cats need grooming?

The Rex cat has a very short layer of wavy fur. Grooming with a comb or brush could scratch the cat's skin, but its fur can be wiped with a chamois leather to keep it soft and silky. The Sphynx cat is virtually hairless, although it does have a down of fine fur on its face, ears, paws, and tail. The skin should be washed with warm water and a sponge.

Feline Facials

With their short noses and "squashed" faces, Persian cats often develop blockages in their tear ducts. This causes their eyes to run, which can discolor the fur around the eyes and on the cheeks. Any unusual discharge from the eyes should be examined by a veterinarian.

Clean the area around the cat's eyes with a cotton ball moistened with warm water. Be careful not to touch the eyeball. To clean the discolored fur, use a cotton ball moistened with a mild salt solution.

Inspect your cat's ears regularly. Dark-colored wax, which may be caused by ear mites and inflammation, should be treated by a veterinarian. For general cleaning, moisten a cotton ball with a little baby oil, and wipe away any dirt on the inside of the cat's ears. Never put anything, such as a cotton swab, into the cat's ears.

A

In the wild, the cat's diet of fresh prey would help to keep its teeth free of tartar and its gums healthy. But cats who have a mainly soft diet, such as canned food, should have their teeth checked regularly to make sure there is no tartar, which builds up around the base of the teeth. Tartar attacks the gums and causes inflammation and infection, which will spread into the root area and can result in severe gum problems and loss of teeth.

To help prevent a buildup of tartar, a cat's teeth should be cleaned about once a week. Always check the gums and mouth generally first, to make sure there is no inflammation or ulcers. If there are, the cat should be taken to a veterinarian. If not, the cat's teeth can be cleaned with a child's toothbrush or a specially made cat toothbrush, using cat toothpaste or a solution of salt and water. Prepare the cat for having its teeth brushed by first examining the teeth gently, and just touching the gums with a soft toothbrush or a cotton swab. Dab a little of the toothpaste on its lips, to help it get accustomed to the taste. If the cat is very distressed at having its teeth cleaned, it may need to visit the veterinarian once a year for a thorough clean and descaling under anesthetic. Ask the veterinarian about alternatives, such as tooth gel, which cats can eat and which acts like a toothpaste without the need to clean the cat's teeth.

Q. Why do I need help

? *Why do you bathe me when I can clean myself?*

Cats don't usually need help in keeping their fur clean, but if the cat's coat is particularly dirty or the cat is longhaired, an occasional bath may be necessary. Fill the bathtub or kitchen sink with about 4 inches (10 cm) of warm water, and gently but firmly place the cat in it. Using a sponge or cup, pour water over the cat's body, avoiding its face and eyes and the top of its head. Gently clean the fur with baby shampoo or special cat shampoo, and rinse with lukewarm water. Lift the cat out of the sink and wrap it in a warm towel. If necessary, gently clean the top of its head and its face with a moistened soft cloth. Towel-dry the cat. Some cats tolerate being dried with a hairdryer, but the noise scares many of them. Keep the cat in a warm room until it is completely dry, then brush or comb the fur.

looking after my teeth?

A Helping Hand

Cats can generally look after themselves perfectly well without the aid of humans. Sometimes, however, the pampered domestic cat can need a little help.

If a cat's fur becomes very matted, take it to a veterinarian, who will sedate the cat and shave off the lumps of fur. Never try to shave the fur yourself.

Cats keep their claws trimmed through the wear and tear of everyday living, but if your cat doesn't go out or is elderly, its claws may need regular clipping. Overgrown claws can grow into the cat's pad, causing infection. Only trim your cat's claws if you have a very steady hand, and if your cat will sit quietly. Otherwise take it to a veterinarian. If you choose to do it yourself, use a pair of claw clippers rather than scissors.

To trim your cat's claws, gently expose them. Each claw has a white tip and a pink quick. The pink quick is where the blood vessels are, and must not be clipped. Remove the white tip in a straight line. Cutting into the quick is painful and will cause bleeding. If you are in doubt, ask your veterinarian to show you how to clip the cat's claws properly.

A tomcat is ruled by its sex drive. Toms are constantly seeking out females in heat, and will travel long distances to find one. The unneutered male is more likely to become involved in a traffic accident, or to get lost as it wanders off in search of a mate. Toms have regular and very aggressive fights, resulting in scratches and bites that can develop into abscesses, which may result in amputation. Eyes and ears are often badly scarred. They are also at risk of contracting viruses, such as feline leukemia and feline AIDS, which are passed from cat to cat in saliva.

Because of their spraying behavior and their tendency to terrorize other cats in the neighborhood, toms are rarely welcome in others people's homes and have few friends, either feline or human. But perhaps the most persuasive argument in favor of neutering is that in a society already overrun with starving and unhealthy groups of feral cats, it is essential that some control is exercised on the cat population, and that the number of unwanted cats being born is kept to a minimum.

why is it important to neuter male cats?

? *What is a neutered male?*

A neutered male is a tomcat that has been castrated (had its testicles removed). A tom can be neutered at any age, but it is best to have it done when the cat is between four and six months old, otherwise behavior patterns become set and will remain even after the operation. Neutering is carried out under anesthetic. It usually requires no stitches, and the cat recovers fully after only a day or two. There are animal welfare organizations and veterinarians who will perform the procedure free or for a reduced fee, in an effort to encourage owners to neuter their cats. Living with an unneutered tom, and the injuries it will sustain, can be a lot more expensive than the neutering operation.

Battle Scars and Spraying

Unneutered tomcats have more aggressive and territorial behavior patterns than their neutered counterparts.

Toms fight each other to mate with a female and to defend their territory, which frequently results in torn ears and a scarred face.

Toms are more aggressive in protecting and marking their territory, which involves spraying a strong-smelling urine both inside and outside the house that can be very difficult to eradicate.

Other injuries sustained by fighting toms are bites to the tail or the base of the back. These bites can easily become infected, and if not treated early enough, can result in part of the tail having to be amputated. In some cases, the tail nerves are damaged and the tail loses all movement.

How do you know when a female cat is ready to mate?

A

A female cat who is ready to mate shows distinct changes in behavior. The cat becomes very affectionate, rubbing against people and things and meowing softly. She is restless, makes loud calling noises, may lose interest in her food, and may urinate more frequently. Neighborhood toms will be attracted by her scent.

? *How many kittens can a female cat have?*

A female cat can become pregnant at the age of six months, and continue to have litters for the next 12 years. During this time, she can give birth to over 200 kittens. The process of giving birth and raising young can be very demanding, and may cause premature aging. A spayed female looks exactly the same as her unspayed counterpart – there is no reason why a spayed cat should put on weight if a proper diet is followed.

? *Should a female be allowed at least one litter before spaying?*

There is no advantage whatsoever in allowing a female cat to have kittens before she is spayed. In fact, the spaying procedure could be marginally more complicated once the female cat has had a litter. Female cats should be spayed when they are five to six months old, to avoid an unwanted pregnancy. Many thousands of unwanted kittens are killed or abandoned every year.

The Mating Game

The courting ritual may take hours, or even days, before the female allows mating to take place.

Before mating, the female rolls around on the ground, rubbing and stretching and making little noises. The male may approach her several times only to be repelled.

When the female is ready for mating, she goes into a characteristic pose, raising her hindquarters and swishing her tail to one side. She paddles with her front feet in an excited manner.

Having gotten the green light, the male mounts the female and grasps the scruff of her neck between his teeth. Copulation is very quick, and ends with a short, sharp scream from the female. This is because the penis has barbs that scratch the female painfully as the penis is withdrawn. It is this action that causes the eggs to be released. After mating, the cats separate and clean themselves, but usually mate again. The female may mate with a number of different toms, resulting in a mixed litter.

A

The average lifespan of a cat is 15 years, but many live for 20 years, and a few even longer. Once they are over the age of 12 (the human equivalent of 75 years old), cats can be considered elderly, and special attention should be paid to their needs. Signs of aging include becoming thinner, less alert and responsive to stimuli, sleeping more, and losing appetite. The cat's coat may become less thick and smooth. The elderly cat may not like to be picked up as much as it used to, or it may want even more comfort and cuddling. An elderly cat does not want too much change in routine, and stays in a kennel should be avoided.

Q. what will i be

like when i'm old ?

? *Will I go gray and deaf, and lose my teeth?*

Some cats do grow gray hairs as they get older, and black cats can get a distinct salt-and-pepper look. The fur of a very black cat lightens over the years, and can end up a reddish-brown color. A cat's hearing and eyesight can deteriorate in the same way as a human's. If the cat's hearing deteriorates, remember that it can't hear warning shouts or the vacuum cleaner creeping up behind it. Owners need to be more vigilant. If the cat's eyesight deteriorates, its food bowls and litterbox should always be kept in the same place, and furniture shouldn't be moved around. The cat's bed should be easy to reach, and the cat should not be let out unsupervised. If the cat has had a mainly soft food diet, it may have a buildup of tartar on its teeth. This will result in loosening of the teeth in the gums, and the teeth will begin to fall out if the tartar is not treated. But if the cat's teeth are looked after, there is no reason why they should fall out just because of old age.

Senior Citizens

An elderly cat should be taken to the veterinarian for regular checkups. The veterinarian can detect any major deterioration in the cat's vital organs, such as heart, brain, liver, and kidneys. There are also a number of ways in which you can make your older cat's life more comfortable.

Keep an eye on your elderly cat's bowel habits, to see if there are any radical changes. An older cat may suffer from constipation; regular meals of sardines, about once a week, or two to three teaspoonfuls of medicinal mineral oil, may help. If the constipation persists for more than a few days, consult with your veterinarian. Diarrhea can be a sign of a tumor in an elderly cat.

If the cat has always slept outside, make a little bed for it indoors, because it may be less eager now to spend the night out carousing.

The older cat needs more grooming. It may need to have its claws trimmed, because it is not rushing around so much, and regular brushing will help it avoid furball. Always brush an elderly cat very gently, and don't pull or twist its legs or body, which could cause discomfort and even injury.

Can you see what I'm feeling by looking at me

What does it mean when I purr

What does it mean when I wag my tail

SPECIAL FEATURE: Understanding a mother cat

Why do I like to be stroked

When I'm being stroked, why do I suddenly attack

What are my whiskers good for

Why do my eyes glow in the dark

What is the flehman reaction

Why do I hunt even though I am well fed

How intelligent am I

Understanding your Cat

Cats can be mysterious and inscrutable, and they are endlessly fascinating to watch. An insight into how your cat thinks and how it perceives the world will help you to understand some of its more baffling behavior, to deal with any stress-related problems that may arise, and to marvel at what a truly superior creature your cat is.

A

Although cats are known for being inscrutable, they give many facial signs that help to convey what they are feeling. Some cats seem to have a permanent expression on their faces, such as a smile, or as with a Burmese, a grouchy look. A cat uses its ears, whiskers, and eyes to show a range of emotions and feelings, from contentment to anger.

Can you see what I'm

? *What* do my eyes tell you?

As in human beings, a cat's pupils dilate or expand, depending on whether it is looking at something it likes or not. The confusing aspect about a cat's pupils, however, is that they expand both when the cat is pleased and when it is afraid. If presented with a huge bowl of its favorite food, a hungry cat's pupils expand rapidly. Similarly, when it feels threatened or scared, a cat's pupils expand, but a cat that is threatening it will have narrowed pupils. When a cat is relaxed, sleepy, and contented, its eyes are often half closed with the pupils dilated. There is an old wives' tale that when a cat blinks at its owner, it is blowing a kiss.

? *What* do my ears and whiskers tell you

A cat with ears facing forward, and with straight and relaxed whiskers, is a happy cat. A cat who is unsure of the situation, but who is not directly threatened, such as one confronted by an energetic toddler, will look alarmed, with its head held stiffly, its ears flattened, its whiskers stiff, and its pupils fully dilated. In this situation, it is probably deciding whether to remain where it is or take flight. A cat engaged in hunting perks up its ears, bristles its whiskers, and has fully dilated pupils.

feeling by looking at me ?

Body Language

A cat's body language can tell you and other cats a lot about how it is feeling and what it is thinking.

A cat is at its most vulnerable when lying stretched out on its back, showing its stomach. A cat that does this, and allows you to stroke its stomach, is a very secure, trusting, and confident cat.

In the home, most cats remain relaxed and content, sitting sphinx-like with their toes tucked under their chest, curled in a ball asleep, or stretched out in their favorite corner.

A

Q. What does it mean when I purr

To a cat lover, the sound of purring is music to the ears. It indicates a happy, peaceful cat, who enjoys being where it is and could wish for nothing better in life. Cats first begin to purr when they are a few days old. Kittens are born blind, so they bond with their mother through her smell. As their senses develop over the first few days of life, they become aware of her purring to them. They then return the purr, usually when suckling, since the kitten can make this bonding noise with its mouth closed. Cats continue to purr throughout their life, especially when contented, when greeting an owner or another cat, and when eating and sleeping, which is why purring has always been associated with a happy, tranquil cat. However, cats have been known to purr when they are hunting, and when they are in pain or distress. Why this is no one knows.

? How do I purr?

If it is a mystery why cats purr, how they purr is an even bigger conundrum. There are two theories. The first is that purring is caused by the vibration of blood passing through a large vein in the cat's chest. The sound of the blood passing through the vein is magnified by the windpipe and air spaces in the cat's skull, and this is what can be heard when a cat purrs. A more probable theory is that the sound is produced in the cat's larynx, by its vocal cords opening and closing.

? Why do I knead with my claws?

Kneading is closely associated with purring, and is usually performed by a contented cat. Kneading is a reversion to kittenhood, when the kitten kneaded its mother's teat to encourage the flow of milk. The kneading was usually accompanied by purring. In adult cats, kneading occurs when they are settling on a lap or preparing a spot for sleep, and is a sign of a relaxed and happy cat.

Top Marks

Cats have many ways of marking their owners and surroundings with their own scent.

A cat has numerous scent glands on its head, just under its chin, around its lips (especially at the corners), and on each side of its forehead, between the eye and the ear. When a cat rubs its head against a piece of furniture or against your hand or cheek, it is leaving a trace of its scent, which marks the furniture and you as part of its territory.

When a cat rubs against your leg affectionately, it is using the scent glands on its face and at the base of its tail to reinforce its smell on you, and to overlay any other scents you may have picked up.

Cats leave a scent behind when they scratch on trees as part of their territorial markings.

what does it mean when I wag my tail

A The belief that cats wag their tails only when they are angry is not entirely true. Cats also wag their tails when they are faced with a dilemma – when they don't know what to do about a situation, or are torn between two options. For example, if a stranger holds out a piece of food to a cat, on one hand the cat will want to take the food, on the other hand it may be unsure about the person offering the food. In this state of indecision, the cat will wag its tail.

A cat uses its tail to help maintain its balance, such as when it is walking along fences or tiptoeing between ornaments on a shelf. If the cat feels itself toppling to one side, it utilizes its tail like a rudder to balance itself. This tail-wagging behavior is transferred to a situation where the cat is torn between two lines of action. The tail-waving helps the cat to keep its balance mentally, while it figures out which way to jump, or which option to take.

? Why do I wag my tail when I'm hunting?

In the wild, a cat hunts undercover, so that only its face can be seen while it stalks its prey through the undergrowth before pouncing. It is unnatural for a cat to hunt in the open. However, most of today's backyards have smooth areas of grass or paving, with little or no undergrowth, so domestic cats must hunt in the open. The cat's desire to chase a bird is as strong as ever, but so is the unease about hunting while in full sight of its prey. Should the cat run and pounce before it is spotted, or should it creep up and then pounce? The state of conflict results in a wagging tail.

Tell Tail Signs

A cat's tail is very flexible, and is used in many different ways to help the cat express a wide range of moods and reactions. It even moves when the cat is asleep.

If the cat holds its tail upright and still when greeting you, this means it is pleased to see you, and is feeling relaxed and comfortable. Often, while the cat is being patted, its tail will quiver. This is a sign of pleasure, acknowledging the human's greeting.

? How would I cope without a tail?

A cat can lose its tail through any number of injuries, and usually adapts to life without a tail quite easily. There are even two tailless breeds of cat, the Manx cat and the Japanese Bobtail. The Manx Rumpy has no tail at all, while the Manx Stumpy has a rudimentary tail. The Japanese Bobtail, as the name suggests, has a short, fluffy tail, which looks similar to a rabbit's.

When pouncing, the tail is kept on the ground to avoid alarming the prey, but the cat's internal conflict at hunting in the open means the tail swishes from side to side.

When a cat is sleeping, the sudden thump of the tip of its tail is a sure sign that it is dreaming.

SPECIAL
FEATURE

Understanding a Mother Cat

Kittens are totally dependent on the mother cat for the first few weeks of their lives, and she will dedicate herself to feeding them and keeping them warm.

The length of a female cat's pregnancy is roughly nine weeks. The first physical signs of pregnancy are a noticeable increase in the pink of her nipples, known as "pinking up." Before this, she may have become less active and eaten less than usual, and like some humans, may even have vomited. After four to five weeks, it is possible to feel the developing fetuses, but avoid handling the cat's abdomen, because this can easily damage the fetuses and cause a miscarriage.

At about the sixth week of pregnancy, the mother's abdomen will be noticeably bigger. At about the seventh week, she starts to become restless, and to search for a place to have her kittens. During the last week of pregnancy, her mammary glands become enlarged, and the nipples very prominent. She may also become withdrawn, and there may be a small amount of white discharge from the vulva. If the cat's abdomen is too big for her to be able to clean her hindquarters, you may need to wipe beneath her tail gently with a cloth soaked in warm water, drying thoroughly afterwards.

Building a Nest

Most pregnant cats devote a great deal of care and effort to choosing a good "nest" for their kittens. The mother's instinct in the

▲ Kittens are born blind and find their way to their mother's milk through smell. Purring also helps to bond mother and kittens.

wild would be to find somewhere safe and secluded where the litter would be out of harm's way. Often, owners prepare boxes and cupboards with blankets and hot water bottles, fluffy toys, and pillows, only for the mother to choose what seems like a particularly dark and uncomfortable spot to have her babies. However, if you put a box filled with newspaper in a warm, quiet spot, and place the mother cat in it regularly, she may well decide to make her nest there. She will begin to shred the newspaper or the cardboard box to make the nest more comfortable.

Many cats instinctively prepare more than one nest, since they will probably move the kittens around, so make sure she doesn't have access to places where a nest would be a problem.

Maternal Instinct

The birth may take up to 24 hours, and the kittens will begin to suckle as soon as the mother has cleaned them. Mother cats may move their litter several times when the kittens are very young. This is a safety measure, in case their squealing has alerted predators to their presence, or in a domestic situation, if there is excessive human interference. Nursing cats are very territorial and protect their kittens fiercely, so keep young children and other animals away from the nesting box until the kittens are at least a week old. Young children should not be encouraged to pick up the kittens. Mother cats become very distressed when a kitten wanders too far or is taken away.

Once the kittens have reached between three and five weeks of age, the mother may begin to avoid them and refuse to feed them, only to resume feeding a few days later. This seemingly unmaternal behavior usually happens with a large litter that the mother feels unable to sustain. She is encouraging the kittens to eat more solid food, and thus reduce her need to feed them.

Many mothers play with their kittens once they are old enough, and it is through play that the kittens learn hunting techniques, and how to relate to the world around them. If the litter is large, the mother might leave the kittens to play together, because it is too tiring for her to play with them all.

▲ Toward the end of her pregnancy, the mother cat may become quiet and withdrawn, and want to be left alone to rest and prepare her nest.

▲ A mother cat teaches her kittens hunting techniques and how to relate to the world around them through play.

The first thing a mother cat does when her kittens are born is to lick them clean. This stroking with the tongue also reassures the blind kittens that mother is there, and creates a bond between them. Mother cats continue to lick their kittens as they grow, especially after they have eaten, and healthy kittens associate this licking with a sense of contentment and well-being. The gentle stroking action of a human being induces the same good feeling. It reminds the cat of its kittenhood and sends it into a sleepy reverie, usually accompanied by purring and paw paddling.

why do I like to be stroked

? *Is* *that also why I like to have my head and face tickled?*

Yes. Cats, both domestic and wild, often greet each other by rubbing heads together. This is a sign of affection and of being at ease with each other, and it reinforces scent bonding. There is also a more practical reason. It is difficult for a cat to reach the top of its head to scratch it, so what better than to get a willing passerby to do it!

The Right Stroke

Stroking a cat is a sign of trust and affection between pet and owner, which also has a positive effect on a human's well-being, helping to lower blood pressure and reduce stress.

Cats love to be stroked on the chest and neck. This is an ideal way to begin stroking a cat who doesn't know you well, since it remains in a position from which it can make a quick getaway if it wants to, but can also enjoy some pampering.

A relaxed cat might lie down and enjoy being stroked down its back. Many cats particularly like being scratched lightly at the base of the tail, as this is a difficult-to-reach area. Always stroke the cat in the direction the fur lies, since many cats do not like to have their fur stroked from the bottom up.

A cat feels very vulnerable when it is exposing its stomach, so it is a sign of trust if a cat lets you stroke it there. Treat the cat gently, because any sudden movement can cause it to panic and scratch or bite.

A

This is common behavior in all cats. One minute the cat is sitting calm and relaxed, purring and content; the next, it lashes out with its claws, or bites at the stroking hand, and flees into a corner. It is thought that this behavior represents a sudden change in how the cat perceives its situation of being stroked, from one of security to one of threat.

Initially, the cat enjoys sitting on a lap being stroked, luxuriating in memories of kittenhood when it was being licked by its mother. Suddenly, as the need to be petted is satisfied, the cat forgets its kittenhood, and feels instead that the stroking hand is attacking or restraining it. The cat becomes defensive, and lashes out at the "enemy" as it leaps off the offending lap. Many cats are just as startled by this sudden change in their behavior as the confused stroker, and will sit looking rather bemused, or clean themselves until they regain their composure. This sudden attack could also be provoked by the cat's memories of being gently stroked before being grabbed to be confined.

The abrupt change in the cat's behavior is more understandable when the cat's stomach is being stroked, because lying on its back is a very vulnerable position for a cat. Sometimes when it is having its stomach stroked, a cat wraps its paws around the hand and bites it, while scraping the hand with its back legs. This is how a cat treats its prey, and is instinctive play behavior, emulating a catch.

? Why do I sometimes lick my nose?

No one knows why for sure, but when a cat feels slightly nervous or uncertain, it flicks its tongue out and touches the tip of its nose. This is a rapid, instinctive reaction to an unsettling or puzzling situation, and could be the feline equivalent of the human frown.

? when I'm

being stroked, why do I suddenly attack

Show of Strength

Cats are very territorial, and protect their territory with frightening displays of aggression and blood-curdling yells and screams. But these are often shows of strength that rarely end in actual fights. Most serious battles take place between intact toms who are preparing to mate.

A cat that feels threatened by another animal, usually a dog, raises its back and tail and fluffs out its fur to make itself look bigger than it really is.

A dominant cat in a fight sits upright and leans forward, with its ears upright and facing forward. It keeps its tail low on the ground, and swishes it from side to side.

A cat cornered by another cat, but not wanting to fight, assumes the submissive position. It crouches low on the ground, flattens its ears and its fur, and seems to be saying, "Don't pick on me, I'm too small." It also holds its tail close to its body, and thumps it on the ground.

A

A cat's whiskers are extremely sensitive, so cats use them for many purposes. At night in dim light, the cat's whiskers act as antennae, and help them to avoid bumping into things. They also help the cat to judge the wind speed and direction before making a big jump. It uses its whiskers to gauge the width of an opening to avoid getting stuck, and its whiskers help it to locate a wind-borne scent, such as that of food or a female in heat. Cats push their whiskers forward to touch prey they have just killed, to check that it is completely dead without having to release it. The whiskers are also used to greet other cats and to show emotions.

what are my

whiskers good for ?

The Cat's Whiskers

? Why do I sometimes race around the house?

This mad-dash behavior is mostly seen in cats that are not allowed outdoors. It is a way of releasing pent-up energy that a cat would normally spend outside, chasing prey, protecting its territory, and generally exploring. It is known as a vacuum activity, and is a way for the cat to satisfy its basic urges to hunt and chase. In its pampered and well-fed state, the domestic cat has little more to do than shuffle toward its food bowl for a ready-made meal, and then decide which chair to curl up on for a snooze. All of the cat's natural energy and tension build up, until suddenly it reaches a critical point. Something triggers the release of this tension, and the cat bounds off, dashing around the house in crazy pursuit of goodness-knows-what. It will then calm down as quickly as it started.

This frantic behavior can also be caused by vibrations in the air, especially if the weather is stormy. Because a cat's whiskers are so sensitive, they can sometimes pick up the vibrations of an impending thunderstorm or heavy winds. Such conditions cause the cat to become greatly agitated, and it may prowl restlessly through the house or dash from room to room, seeking refuge. It is said that cats can predict earthquakes and tornadoes because they feel the vibrations before humans. In many countries, when their cat starts to behave in a restless and agitated way, the owners prepare themselves for possible extreme weather.

It is not surprising that something superlatively good is sometimes termed "the cat's whiskers," because they are a remarkable piece of equipment. Without its whiskers, technically known as *vibrissae*, the cat would be at a great loss.

Cats don't only have whiskers on their faces. There is another set on the back of each foreleg. These are known as carpal hairs, and are just as sensitive.

Many cats have "whiskers" for eyebrows, which continually fall out and regrow.

Different breeds of cat have different whiskers. The Devon Rex (above) has short, curly whiskers, whereas the American Wirehair (left) has coarse, wiry, crimped whiskers.

A

Just behind the cat's retina is a membrane known as the tapetum lucidum, which consists of up to 15 layers of special cells that reflect the light. When a light is shone into the cat's eyes, it is reflected by the tapetum, which is a greenish-yellow color. It is this reflection that can be seen when a cat's eyes glow green or gold in the dark. Humans do not have this membrane, but most mammals do.

? *If it were pitch black, would I be able to see?*

Contrary to popular belief, cats cannot see in the dark, that is, they cannot see in pitch blackness. A cat's eye works much like a human's. When there is bright light, the pupil gets smaller to restrict the amount of light entering the eye; when it is darker, the pupil expands to allow in the maximum amount of light. The pupils in a cat's eyes open much wider than a human's, which means more light enters the eye in dimly lit conditions. This means that cats can see better than humans in lower light levels, but they cannot see in complete darkness.

why do my eyes glow in the dark

Sweet Dreams

Cats sleep more than any other mammals – on average 16 hours a day. But the cat's brain remains just as active asleep as it is awake, and a cat can react to external stimulation immediately from a deep sleep.

Watching a cat while it is asleep will leave you in no doubt that cats dream. The tip of the tail thumping gently is a sure sign that the cat is chasing something.

? Can I see the same colors that you see?

It was once thought that cats could only see in black, white, and gray, but research has shown that cats can see a limited range of colors. Cats have been trained to discriminate between colors, essentially, green and blue. However, it is thought that cats cannot discriminate between different color values, and that variations in color don't mean much to them.

A cat's paws and whiskers also twitch when it dreams. It might even make little noises.

Cats choose warm, safe places in which to sleep. A cat might curl up next to a baby because of the body warmth, but this must be discouraged, because the cat might inadvertently suffocate the baby by lying on top of it, or scratch the baby if he or she makes a sudden movement.

A

When a cat detects a particularly interesting or pungent smell, it raises its head, opens its mouth, and draws back its lips in what looks like a grimace of horror. This is known as flehming, and the cat is actually tasting the smell that it is picking up. The cat draws in air through its open mouth into a cavity just behind the first incisor teeth, where there is an organ known as Jacobson's organ. This enables the cat to get a really good smell of the scent in the air.

What is the flehman reaction

? *How good is my sense of smell?*

Cats have a much better sense of smell than humans, but it is not as good as a dog's sense of smell. Some dogs have up to 150 million nerve endings in their nose, while cats have about 20 million and humans 5 million. A cat uses its heightened sense of smell for many purposes. A blind, newborn kitten is guided to its mother's nipples by her smell, and this also helps the kitten to find her if it strays. As a cat grows older, it uses scent from one of its scent glands to mark its territory, and to sniff out the scent of other cats. Cats smell their food carefully before eating to check that it is all right, which is why stale food left in the bowl, or lingering smells from disinfectant, can easily put a cat off its food. Toms can detect a female in heat over an amazingly long distance because of her sexual scent, which is why such a cat will always have a circle of admirers.

Common Scents

The smells humans carry around with them give cats all sorts of information, such as where they have been and if they have met any other cats.

A visitor who comes to the house should always greet the resident cat with an extended hand. The cat will sniff the person's fingers, and note his or her individual scent to see whether this is someone it has previously encountered, in which case it will allow itself to become more friendly.

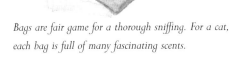

Bags are fair game for a thorough sniffing. For a cat, each bag is full of many fascinating scents.

Friendly cats often greet each other by sniffing and licking each other's face. A cat will do this naturally with a favored human.

A

Cats are hunters first and pets second. No matter how well fed, petted, or pampered a cat is, its instinct to hunt will remain strong and persistent. The only difference is that a well-fed cat may not eat its prey, while a hungry or wild cat devours it on the spot. In the wild, cats mostly hunt rodents, but a domestic cat hunts most creatures smaller than itself, such as frogs, birds, voles, squirrels, young rabbits, and even insects. Cats generally prefer to hunt at night, but will hunt at any time, even after a full meal. This may be because in the wild a cat would catch just enough for one small meal and then quickly go on to its next catch – it couldn't afford to wait until it was hungry again before hunting its next meal. Observation has shown that cats who are not desperately hungry are actually more efficient at hunting, probably because they are more relaxed and less anxious to catch the prey to satisfy their hunger.

? _Why_ do I bring my prey home?

This is a cat's way of telling its owners that they are not very good hunters. The cat is offering its catch as a tasty morsel, since its owners are obviously incapable of catching their own mice. Mother cats bring home their prey to teach their kittens how to hunt, and this behavior in a neutered female may be a reflection of that instinct.

why do i hunt even

? *Why do I play with my prey?*

Cats often toss their prey in the air, bat it about on the ground, and shake it between their teeth before killing it. Although humans are horrified by this behavior, the cat is not aware that it is being cruel and causing pain. It is not deliberately torturing its prey. The playing probably helps the cat to release tension after the intense and controlled stalking of the prey. Many predators, including dogs, shake their prey to kill it by breaking its back.

Hunting Techniques

Although cats have a strong instinct to hunt, they do not instinctively know how to do so. They must be taught as kittens. If a kitten is not shown how to hunt by its mother, it will never learn. In the wild, a mother cat would bring home real prey to teach her kittens, but for domestic cats, a toy mouse is a more acceptable substitute.

A kitten learns to ambush its prey by creeping up on it, with its body close to the ground.

The kitten will then pounce on the toy mouse. At this point, it will often play with the prey, tossing it up in the air or batting it from paw to paw on the ground.

The final killing bite to the back of the neck is a learned technique. If the kitten is not taught this by its mother, it will never do it instinctively, and will therefore never be able to kill its prey.

...hough I am well fed

A It is pointless to compare a cat's intelligence to a human's, but as animals who can adapt to their surroundings, fend for themselves in hostile environments, and turn situations to their own advantage, cats are very intelligent. Cats are keen observers, and they are also curious. A cat will wait until its owner's back is turned before snatching the sausages from the kitchen table; it will quickly recognize that the sound of the can opener or rattle of a box means food, and that the squeal of a young child is a signal to flee or hide under the nearest table. As survivors, they are superior to dogs, because they are much more independent, and more adept at begging for food and scavenging. Cats are also cautious, and often sit back and size up a situation before deciding which course of action to take – and once they have decided, it will usually be to their own benefit!

How

? *Do I have a sixth sense?*

Because of their association with witches and magic, their haughty independence, and some spectacular feats they have performed over the decades, cats are often thought to have mystical powers. There are many stories about cats finding their way home across thousands of miles, rescuing babies from certain death in the middle of the night, and suddenly raising their hackles for no apparent reason. But many of these actions happen because of the cat's natural makeup rather than ESP.

It is thought that cats can find their way home by an innate homing sense that is common in many animals and birds, especially those that migrate. Sudden dramatic yowlings and hissings in the middle of the night are because the cat's heightened senses can detect the smallest sounds and movements, not because there's a poltergeist moving the furniture around downstairs. In the case of cats who woke up their owners in the middle of the night by a constant meowing, just in time for them to stop their baby from suffocating, this is because the baby's struggles disturbed the cat, which was alarmed by the change in routine rather than a knowing desire to alert the parents to the distress of their child.

intelligent am I

Cats learn to open doors using the handle by watching their owners.

Cats learn that tasty things are often kept in bowls or pitchers, and when no one is looking, explore their contents.

Learning Curve

Cats are difficult to train because they are so independent, and because they have no inherent desire to please their owners. However, cats are capable of learning, usually by watching carefully and then repeating the movement, much as a kitten learns to hunt.

Cats can be taught to beg like a dog, but only do so because they want the food, not to entertain the crowds.

Symptoms and Ailments

Most well-cared-for domestic cats live a long and healthy life – or even nine! If something does go wrong, however, prompt action by the owner could mean the difference between life and death. In some situations, such as an accident or viral infection, a cat's system reacts rapidly, and the cat could deteriorate very quickly. In other situations, an owner's careful observations of the cat can provide the veterinarian with much essential information.

This section gives a list of symptoms, together with possible ailments and suggestions of what owners should do. There is also a code indicating how serious the symptoms are. Remember, though, if the cat is in pain or distress, or if you are unsure what is wrong, take the cat to the veterinarian immediately.

KEY

Keep cat under observation for 3–4 days. If symptoms persist, make an appointment with the veterinarian.

Keep cat under observation for 24–48 hours. If symptoms do not improve, contact veterinarian.

Take cat to veterinarian if there is no improvement within 12 hours, or if condition worsens.

Take cat to veterinarian immediately. This is an emergency.

SYMPTOM	POSSIBLE CAUSES	OWNER ACTION	KEY
ABDOMINAL DISTENSION	Pregnancy, fluid in abdomen	Check for other signs, such as nipple enlargement, poor appetite	● ●
ALOPECIA	Allergic skin disease, excessive grooming, infection with mites or fungi, hormonal problem	Observe for licking and scratching	●
APPETITE *Increase in*	Increased activity, overactive thyroid gland, diabetes, tumor	Measure daily food intake and discuss with veterinarian	●
Loss of	Fever, infection, pain, stress, gastro-intestinal disorder, kidney failure, sore mouth	Take temperature. Check mouth	● ●
BAD BREATH	Dental disease, gastrointestinal disorder, worms	Check teeth and gums. Look for signs of worms	●
BEHAVIORAL CHANGES	Pain, metabolic disease, central nervous system disease, stress	Observe cat for any unusual physical signs	●
BITE WOUNDS	Fight with another cat, or a rat or dog	Bathe with saline solution and take to veterinarian for a course of antibiotics	● ● ●
BLEEDING *From mouth*	Trauma, foreign body, dental disease	Check teeth. Check for foreign body	● ● ●
From nose	Trauma, foreign body, tumor	Observe for sneezing and check if there is any swelling on face	● ● ●

Symptom	Possible causes	What to do	
In feces	Colitis, enteritis, constipation	Note if cat squats frequently	● ● ●
In urine	Cystitis, bladder stones, tumor	Note cat's position when urinating	● ● ● ●
BREATHING *Difficult/distressed*	Trauma, ruptured diaphragm, air or fluid in pleural space, collapsed lung	Keep cat quiet. Do not lay cat on its side or back	● ● ● ●
Noisy	Feline asthma, partial airway obstruction	Observe whether cat has difficulty breathing	● ● ● ●
Rapid	Fright, hemorrhage, oxygen shortage	Keep cat quiet in well-ventilated area. Do not attempt to hold or cuddle cat	● ● ● ●
COMA/LOSS OF CONSCIOUSNESS	Trauma, brain disease, diabetes	Keep cat warm and ensure airway is clear	● ● ● ●
CONSTIPATION	Inadequate fluid intake, bowel problem	Observe whether cat is passing urine. NB: if frequent squatting, contact veterinarian immediately	● ● ●
CONVULSIONS	Epilepsy, poisoning, kidney failure	Check mouth and fur for poison. Keep cat in a safe environment	● ● ● ●
COORDINATION, LOSS OF	Shock, fractures, metabolic disease, spinal cord or brain trauma or disease, poison	Keep cat warm	● ● ● ●
COUGH	Infection, lungworm, foreign body, furball	Observe breathing when cat is at rest	● ● ●

DIARRHEA	Gastrointestinal disorder, parasites, poison	Check mouth for burns and feces for blood. Feed bland diet	● ●
DISCHARGE *Ear*	Infection of ear canal	Avoid touching ear, which can be extremely sore	● ● ●
Eye	Conjunctivitis	Wipe eyes with lukewarm boiled water	● ●
Nose	Upper respiratory illness, rhinitis, foreign body	Note whether discharge from one or both nostrils	● ●
Vagina	Genitourinary infection	Note whether cat urinates frequently	● ● ●
DRINKING EXCESSIVELY	Kidney problem, diabetes	Keep indoors and measure fluid intake	● ●
EAR *Held down*	Infection	Check ears, gently, for signs of infection	● ●
Scratching	Infection, flea allergy, ear mites	Check for smell and discharge	● ●
Smell	Infection	Check ears, gently, for signs of discharge	● ●
EATING, DIFFICULTY IN	Sore gums, broken or loose tooth, fractured jaw, sore or swollen tongue	Look in mouth	● ●

EYE *Change of iris color*	Uveitis, aging, tumor	Check for other symptoms	● ●
Discharge	Conjunctivitis	Bathe eyes with plain, boiled water	● ●
Opaque	Corneal problem, cataract	Keep cat in a safe environment, because its impaired eyesight can put it at risk	● ● ●
Partially closed	Inflammation, pain, foreign body	Check for scratches and obvious foreign bodies	● ● ●
Red	Inflammation of conjunctiva, blood in the eye	Note which parts of eyes are red	● ●
Third eyelid up	Problem in the eye, general ill-health	Check for any injuries and other symptoms	● ●
Weepy/wet	Irritation, poor tear drainage	Clean eyes	●
FACE *Scabs*	Solar dermatitis, skin cancer of ears and nose of white cats, allergic skin disease	Look for fleas	●
Swelling	Abscess, tumor	Palpate to see if painful	● ●
FUR *Dry and dull*	Hormonal imbalance, dietary deficiency, general ill-health	Discuss with veterinarian	●

Symptom	Possible cause	Action	Severity
Falling out	Shedding	Groom cat regularly, especially a longhair. Treat for furball if necessary	●
GROOMING EXCESSIVELY	Itchy skin, behavioral problem	Observe for scratching and flea dirt	●
GUMS, INFLAMED OR BLEEDING	Dental disease, viral infection	Feed soft food	● ●
HEAD *Shaking*	Ear infection, ear mites, foreign body in ear	Check ear for wax and discharge	● ●
Tilting	Ear disease, neurological problem, brain tumor	Observe for other symptoms	● ● ●
LAMENESS *Acute*	Trauma, fracture, sprain, bite wound	Keep cat under observation	● ● ●
Chronic	Arthritis, muscle disease	Observe to see how many limbs are affected	●
LETHARGY	Many causes, eg, infection, heart disease	Check temperature and note any other symptoms	● ●
MAMMARY GLANDS, SWELLING OF	Lumps, tumor, mastitis	Check if painful	● ●
MOUTH *Dribbling*	Gum disease, ulcers, poison, foreign body, viral infection	Check inside mouth	● ●

Pawing at	Object stuck in mouth, loose tooth	Check inside mouth	● ● ●
Sore lips	Eosinophilic ulcer	Look to see extent of sore areas	● ●
NOSE, SNUFFLY	Upper respiratory tract viral infection	Keep nose clean	● ●
PANTING	Overheating, general distress	Treat for overheating. If no change within an hour, take to veterinarian	● ● ●
PARALYSIS	Trauma, neurological disorder, aortic embolism	Keep cat still and calm	● ● ● ●
REGURGITATION	Eating food too quickly, esophageal disease	Feed four or five small meals a day	●
SKIN *Itchy*	Allergic skin disease, fleas, mites	Look for signs of parasites	●
Lumps	Cyst, neoplasm	Observe rate of growth	●
Spots and scabs	Infection, flea bite hypersensitivity	Look for fleas	●
Swelling	Abscess, insect sting	Look for bite wounds	● ●

SNEEZING *With discharge*	Upper respiratory illness, rhinitis	Keep under observation. Check temperature	● ●
Without discharge	Irritation, chlamydia	Watch for discharge	●
SPRAYING	Behavioral problem often associated with presence of other cats	Observe whether cat is spraying or urinating	●
SQUATTING FREQUENTLY	Cystitis, blocked urethra	Keep cat confined with litter box	● ● ● ●
STRAINING TO DEFECATE	Cystitis, block urethra, constipation	Check feces for blood and consistency	● ● ● ●
TEMPERATURE, RAISED	Infection, leukemia	Take temperature	● ● ●
URINATION, EXCESSIVE	Kidney disease, diabetes, urinary tract infection	Ensure plenty of water available to cat	● ● ●
VOMITING	Dietary indiscretion, furball, infection, poison, gastritis	If poison is possible, take to veterinarian immediately; otherwise observe	● ●
WEIGHT *Gain*	Overfeeding, reduced exercise, steroid therapy, pregnancy	Weigh cat weekly and measure food intake	●
Loss	Underfeeding, loss of appetite, difficulty eating, diabetes, impaired digestion and absorption, hyperthyroidism, tumor	Observe for other signs	●

Index